PORTLAND, OREGON
Food Crawls

Eric & Nicole Gitenstein, Mr. & Mrs. MF Tasty

TOURING *the* NEIGHBORHOODS
ONE BITE *&* LIBATION *at a* TIME

Globe
Pequot

GUILFORD, CONNECTICUT

Globe
Pequot

An imprint of The Rowman & Littlefield Publishing Group, Inc.
4501 Forbes Blvd., Ste. 200
Lanham, MD 20706
www.rowman.com

Distributed by NATIONAL BOOK NETWORK

British Library Cataloguing in Publication Information available

Library of Congress Cataloging-in-Publication Data available

ISBN 978-1-4930-4568-6 (paper : alk. paper)
ISBN 978-1-4930-4569-3 (epub)

♾™ The paper used in this publication meets the minimum requirements
of American National Standard for Information Sciences—Permanence of
Paper for Printed Library Materials, ANSI/NISO Z39.48-1992

This book is dedicated to all the lauded spots, but more importantly all the hidden gems, that make Portland as tasty as it is. To all the food friends we've made and all the ones we've yet to meet.

Contents

Introduction

Oh Portland! Your love affair with this city may have already begun, and we expect this book will make you fall even harder. You may hear Portland referred to by other names, including PDX, Bridge City, Drip City, Rip City, Stumptown, Beervana, or the City of Roses. Whatever you choose to call it, you are in for a tasty time. This fun, quirky city has built its reputation on not only "Keeping Portland Weird," but also its booming culinary and beverage scene. You will be hard pressed to find a place that doesn't offer something distinct, mouthwatering, and memorable.

Feasting like royalty is not just for the elite in Portland. You can get an affordable five-star meal in the most unassuming spot, from food carts aplenty (nearly 900) to neighborhood bars that are upping the ante in the kitchen. By law any establishment serving alcohol has to serve what is considered a "full menu," offering at least five items; in other words, in this city if the bar is open, the kitchen is open, and yeah, it's most likely serving something local. Each neighborhood has its own identity with a variety of eateries sure to please all palates. The city is constantly evolving, and there is always something new to stumble upon and explore for tourists and locals alike.

Portland is first divided into four quadrants: Northeast, Southeast, Southwest, and Northwest. It also has what's referred to as the "Fifth Quadrant," North Portland. Beyond that you'll hear references to different neighborhoods and districts. It's a pretty big little city that allows entrepreneurs and artists to draw their own map. Plan on driving out of Portland proper if you want run-of-the-mill chain restaurants, but let's hope that's not what you're here for!

So in a city with so much food noise how does one hear about the spots that are really setting themselves apart and going the extra mile to give you a unique dining experience? We made it our mission to shine a light on spots that usually do not make those trending lists but still pump out those flavor fireworks. In this ever-changing culinary scene, places are constantly opening, but not all make it: Here are the places that stood out during our research. Now go out there and choose tasty over basic!

Follow the Icons

 If you eat something outrageous and don't take a photo for Instagram, did you really eat it? These restaurants feature dishes that are Instagram famous. These items must be seen (and snapped) to be believed, and luckily they taste as good as they look!

 Cheers to a fabulous night out in Portland! These spots add a little glam to your grub and are perfect for marking a special occasion.

 Follow this icon when you're crawling for cocktails. This symbol points out the establishments that are best known for their great drinks. The food never fails here, but make sure to come thirsty, too!

 This icon means that sweet treats are ahead. Bring your sweet tooth to these spots for dessert first (or second, or third).

 Portland is for brunch. Look for this icon when crawling with a crew that needs sweet and savory (or an excuse to drink before noon).

THE ST. JOHNS CRAWL

1. **GRACIE'S APIZZA**, 8737 N. Lombard St., (971) 512-0007, 24thandmeatballs.com

2. **SLIM'S COCKTAIL BAR & RESTAURANT**, 8635 N. Lombard St., (503) 286-3854, www.slimspdx.weebly.com

3. **TIENDA Y TAQUERIA SANTA CRUZ**, 8630 N. Lombard St., (503) 286-7302, tiendasantacruz.com

4. **GABAGOOL**, 7955 N. Lombard St., (503) 894-9096, gabagoolpdx.com

St. Johns

The tip of the city beaming
with small-town charm

THE BEACON OF NORTH PORTLAND, OTHERWISE KNOWN AS Portland's "Fifth Quadrant," St. Johns is on the tip of the peninsula formed by the convergence of the Willamette River and the Columbia River. It blends small-town charm with gems ranging in cuisine, while remaining accessible to its diverse residents. With food ranging from East Coast Italian comfort classics to a taqueria tucked away in a corner market, this neighborhood has a variety of food to pique one's interest. If libations are your primary focus, several different types of bars are within walking distance of one another, including one of the oldest bars in Portland that opened over a century ago. Maybe it's because parking is still abundant, unlike a lot of areas of town, or maybe it's the new wave of residents and their influence, but the times are changing in this once sleepy neighborhood, offering more options to keep the neighborhood locals happy and creating a buzz that is putting this part of Portland on locals' and tourists' radars alike.

1

GRACIE'S APIZZA
Is that a typo or did they mean to write *APizza*? Shouldn't it be just *Pizza*? For those not in the know, it happens to be the name of one of the East Coast's most sought after styles of 'za. New Haven, Connecticut, transplant Craig Melillo is here to spread the gospel of APizza, and after dining at **GRACIE'S**, you will be a believer. New Haven–style pizza is coal fired and has a charred bottom, a slight chew to the dough, and a rustic oblong shape to the pies; no one is striving for that perfect circle but they get pretty close. Melillo uses dough that is naturally leavened from a starter, flour from Cairn Springs Mill in Washington, and swaps out the traditional coal-fired oven for a wood-fired one; all play parts in the distinct flavors at Gracie's.

While ranch does not exist here, you can find some excellent dipping sauces. A house-made hot sauce has a Calabrian chile base with other ingredients rotating with each batch, giving each its own individual taste. Caramelized garlic vinaigrette created for the sole reason of dunking your crust leaves you wondering why no one has thought of this before.

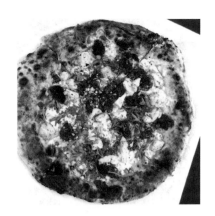

The restaurant is named after Craig's grandmother, and the level of hospitality achieved at Gracie's will remind you of going to Grandma's for dinner. Guests feel well taken care of in the intimate space. Choose from a handful of tables indoors after placing your order at the counter, or opt for the unique covered outdoor patio where guests can enjoy their pizza by the expansive fireplace sheltered from the elements. A well-curated list of interesting, rotating beers and wines are available by the glass or the bottle. While specials and toppings can change with the seasons, the quality of everything always stays top-notch at Gracie's.

2

SLIM'S COCKTAIL BAR & RESTAURANT

This local institution has not lost one bit of its old-school Portland charm since it started serving St. Johns in 1911. Perhaps **SLIM'S** home outside the central evolving landscape of inner Portland helps keep it safely authentic. It's rumored that back in the day, dockworkers would have their paychecks cashed at the small window in front before they spent it inside at the bar. You'll find everyone in the neighborhood, from sports fans watching the game to a younger crowd dancing to their DJ nights, as well as live music, karaoke, bingo, and open mic nights spread

throughout the week. This bar and lounge seems to rarely sleep—it's only closed for a few hours before it opens back up in the wee hours. You'll

be hard pressed to find a better Bloody Mary served at almost any time of the day. Even if you make it during the middle of the afternoon, pinball machines, a pool table, and video lottery can keep you entertained if the TVs aren't showing something that catches your interest. Slim's offers anything you could want from your classic dive bar, but they specialize in creating and curing hangovers.

3

TIENDA Y TAQUERIA SANTA CRUZ

Originally opened as a bakery and meat market in 2000, **TIENDA Y TAQUERIA** expanded its offerings to a restaurant. It's not quite a taco speakeasy, but tucked in the back of this Mexican market and bakery is a taco shop that everyone seems to have heard makes the best tacos in Portland. Simply decorated aside from a fantastic mural that takes up most of one of the walls, the focus is clearly on the food. The menu consists mostly of tacos, tortas, and burritos with your choice of meat. Options

range from the more familiar offerings like carne asada to something more adventurous like *lengua* (beef tongue) or *cabeza* (all the meat from the head of the cow), as well as vegetarian options. A salsa station lets guests choose how much they would like to spice up their meal—the avocado-tomatillo salsa is their standout fan favorite. It's amazing on chips, tacos, or even a spoon, but it especially makes the carne asada in the Tienda Burrito pop.

TIP

If you see churros being offered, get them!

The front of the shop offers many Mexican goods such as hard-to-find candies, spices, desserts like pan dulces and churros, in addition to the staple grocery items found in Mexican cuisine. They're open every day from 7 a.m. to 10 p.m.

4 GABAGOOL

GABAGOOL is a food cart success story. The two East Coast founders, Ryan and Pete, went brick and mortar in 2016 after three years on the street. Gabagool is East Coast slang for the cured meat capicola. Striving to provide a casual, affordable dining experience, this simple and sleekly decorated brand new restaurant space that the owners built to spec has chosen to forgo the traditional linen and table service to focus on procuring the highest quality ingredients either locally or imported directly from Italy.

Gabagool offers a variety of pastas from daily scratch-made dough: hand formed, rested, and rolled in-house. Piadina sandwiches, made with an unleavened flatbread commonly found in the northern Italian region of

Emilia-Romagna but rarely found on a menu in Portland, make several appearances on the menu. Specials rotate frequently but come back around fairly quickly as they know what their regulars look forward to. They offer a full bar serving Italian and Oregon beers, wines, and specialty cocktails; there is something to satisfy almost anyone without breaking the bank. The seasonally changing gnocchi varies depending on what their farmers offer them, but regardless of time of year, this dish has been one of their standouts from their food cart days. One wintertime gnocchi variation involves a rich gorgonzola sauce that hugs you from the inside like you want a warm dish to on a cold winter night. Its loyal following is always hungry for what Chef Ryan will come up with next. Pro-tip: Once you've placed your first order, you can keep your tab open and order additional drinks from your table without having to get up and go to the back of the line.

The Early Bird Gets the Worm

Guests who arrive in the morning can catch that day's fresh pasta hanging on racks in their open kitchen.

THE MISSISSIPPI AVE CRAWL

1. **LIBERTY GLASS**, **938 N. Cook St.**, (503) 517-9931, libertyglass.com

2. **WOLF & BEAR'S**, **3925 N. Mississippi Ave.**, (503) 453-5044, eatwolfandbears.com

3. **QUAINTRELLE**, **3936 N. Mississippi Ave.**, (503) 200-5787, quaintrelle .co

4. **RADAR RESTAURANT**, **3951 N. Mississippi Ave.**, (503) 841-6948, radarpdx.com

5. **INTERURBAN**, **4057 N. Mississippi Ave.**, (503) 284-6669, interurbanpdx.com

6. **PROST FOOD CARTS**, **4237 N. Mississippi Ave.**, (503) 954-2674, prostportland.com

Mississippi Ave

From historic to hipster, dense with shopping, eating, and drinking

WITH SALTWATER AQUARIUMS, VINTAGE KEYBOARD SHOPS, and more restaurants, bars, and breweries stuffed into a few blocks than some midsized cities, Mississippi Ave has enough options to get lost and found a few times over. The area is so photogenic it has been used as a backdrop for such movies as Reese Witherspoon's *Wild*, as well as the HBO series *Here and Now*, and even the show that parodies the city, *Portlandia*. Tourists can explore the historic neighborhood, getting those hard to find vintage lightbulbs from the country's most extensive lightbulb shop (Sunlan Lighting), or pick up a unique piece of print art sourced solely from independent makers at Land Gallery, all while having a taste bud overload from the many food and drink options densely packed within easy walking distance.

1

LIBERTY GLASS

For 10 years, the formerly bubble-gum pink (now black and white) house at the bottom of the hill has been serving up cocktails with a side of charm. Rose and Jason McCormick are siblings who pay homage to the bar their grandparents operated in Fremont, Ohio, in the 1930s. Family owned and operated, **LIBERTY GLASS** serves the neighborhood every night, offering events like Monday night bingo or Sunday spaghetti. Affordable cocktails complement the accessible comfort food. The nachos are the standout bar snack, and you can get them half off at happy hour. Remnants of the space being a former home add to its charm. The claw foot tub in the upstairs bathroom is a great spot for a unique bathroom selfie; don't get any ideas because the faucet has been removed (leave your bath accessories at home). The decor upstairs will make anyone feel comfortable, whether you are an aspiring writer working on your new masterpiece or just dropping in

for an after work drink; there is even a closet turned booth for two customers looking to get extra cozy. The main floor and outdoor patio are great for people watching or meeting your new drinking buddy. Whatever space catches your interest, this converted house makes all their patrons feel like they are at home.

2

WOLF & BEAR'S

WOLF & BEAR'S offers a concise menu of vegetarian-focused Middle Eastern food while offering a vegan substitute for practically every option. Since opening in 2009, Wolf (Tanna Ten-Hoopen Dolinsky) and Bear (Jeremy Garb) have garnered a loyal following of die-hard fans. The signature falafel is grilled instead of being deep fried, which give them a lighter, grease-free texture. The menu is divided into two main sections: pitas and bowls. With over 10 add-ons you can customize your hummus bowl, house salad, or pita to your heart's desire. The much-praised Sabich is a clever combo of sliced hard-boiled egg, hummus, eggplant, potato, onions, and crisp cucumbers folded in a pita with tangy *amba* (a mango pickle condiment), a great bite morning, noon, or night. The cheap eats option is titled "The

Roadside Snack"—with your choice of *lebnah* (a cheese made from strained yogurt) or hummus and two add-ons topped with za'atar spice and olive oil, a filling meal just under $6. One of their most popular dishes is their falafel pita, which con-

Wolf & Bear's is one of the longest-running food carts in Portland.

sists of hummus, grilled onions, roasted red peppers, grilled eggplant, and falafel stuffed into a warm pita to enjoy on the go while walking down the street soaking in the rest of Mississippi Avenue, or in their intimate covered seating area. With light bites that are light on the wallet, Wolf and Bear's is a perfect stop to refuel before the next adventure.

3

QUAINTRELLE

This seasonally focused restaurant works with a range of Oregon purveyors to maximize the local impact of each plate. QUAINTRELLE's lofty standards don't stop with the cuisine; they extend to a beverage program that has earned the Wine Spectator Award of Excellence, as well as the Oregon Wine A-List awards for 2017 and 2018.

Regardless of whether you choose dinner, happy hour, or the chef's $65 tasting menu option, the pricing is extremely reasonable given the high quality of product used. While it does not claim to be a vegetarian restaurant, it is definitely a restaurant that will have you happy to eat your vegetables. Happy hour is from 5 to 6:30 p.m., as well as the last hour of business each day, and 5 to 9 p.m. on Sundays.

While options vary with the seasons, there are typically 10 to 12 food offerings as well as daily rotating classic cocktails and shots. Their rotating Prohibition Punch and daily classic cocktail are two happy hour drink

specials that are not to be missed. Wind down on Wine Wednesday with half off select bottles (wine always seems better when it is half off). If you are not just popping in for a quick bite and drink, this food tastes even better at a leisurely pace, and why not throw in a bottle of wine while you are at it. The kitchen and bar staff effortlessly flow with a common theme of utilizing the best each season has to offer. Bar manager Camille Cavan has been there from the start, and you can often find her behind the bar ready to guide you through the bevy of beverages offered. Chef Riley Erickson and team have brought new life to the kitchen, raising their already high standards. The restaurant itself manages to have a sleek design while still feeling warm and inviting. Pictures of some of the local products at their source adorn the walls, paying homage to their suppliers. You would never know this once housed a build your own mac-and-cheese shop.

With a large floor plan, guests can sit at the wrap-around bar with gorgeous wooden countertop, or be seated at one of the tables on either the first or second floor. If you want to taste Oregon in your glass and on your plate, this is one of the best places to do it. As pretentious as this concept sounds, they humbly deliver it without any sort of pretense.

4

RADAR RESTAURANT

RADAR is a one-of-a-kind neighborhood gem owned by husband and wife team chef Jonathan Berube and Lily Tollefsen. It combines Mid-Atlantic and American bistro cuisine with responsibly sourced ingredients from all that Oregon has to offer. Named after Lily's father (Skip "Radar" Tollefson), their full-service restaurant and bar offers a menu that is unique and approachable, inspired by their coastal culinary experiences. Originally a dinner-only spot, as that is all they could afford to staff, hours have expanded with their success, and every once in a while Jonathan and Lily now can afford a day off! Daily happy hour from 5 to 6 p.m. offers a variety of dishes ranging from snacks to full-sized entrees, with something to satisfy almost any dietary restriction without sacrificing flavor.

Not to be missed are the bluefish pâté, when available, and the chowder fries. Brunch time is the right time to visit as there are almost as many options on the menu as there are seats: 20 and counting. For those looking to pair a drink with any of these dishes, the outstanding beverage program was designed by Lily in collaboration with her longtime friend Alex Day of the highly regarded bar Death & Co. in New York.

Radar houses an entirely open kitchen where guests are offered a chance to watch the chefs in action. With it being such a cozy spot, almost everyone gets a front-row seat. If you want space for a special occasion, you can reserve the private dining room. Whether a date night or a gathering with friends, set your course to Radar for a fun, flavorful time.

5

INTERURBAN

Opened in 2011, **INTERURBAN** is a two-story saloon named after the line of electric trains that used to run throughout the Portland metro area in the first half of the 20th century. Offering a full bar that focuses on pre–Prohibition era cocktails including an extensive whiskey list, there is a cocktail for all palates, as well as a small but focused beer list. Chef Jonny Henry offers seasonally focused pub fare with an emphasis on local game. The crowd favorite is their wild boar burger featuring Los Roast's (Portland's New Mexico hatch green chile connection) peppers, fried onions, *queso botanero*, pickled jalapeños, and aioli.

Open seven nights a week, the space boasts an expansive back patio that is sunny in the summertime and features roaring fire pits in the winter, making for the perfect setting for an outdoor meal or cocktail under the stars. After 11 p.m. a concise late night menu is offered for those who want to keep noshing 'til last call. Weekend brunch is the only time they are open in the daytime, luring the hung over and hungry for dishes like rabbit hash, oysters, and classics like eggs Benedict.

6

PROST FOOD CARTS

To try some of the best Portland food carts all in one place, look no further than the **PROST** beer hall and their attached food cart pod, Prost Marketplace, or as the locals refer to it, the Prost pod. From some of the most popular Texas-style barbecue in the city (Matt's BBQ) to vegan delights (Native Bowl) and everything in between like sushiritos (Teppanyaki Hut) and the legendary Pastrami Zombie, this pod has an option for everyone. Some international standouts include DesiPDX and White Elephant Asian Fusion.

White Elephant's claim to fame is not so much a specific dish, but more the abundance of sauces to choose from for their popular chicken wings. They have been known to receive large orders from the NBA's Portland Trailblazers. Nipping right at the heels to be the number one contender is their Pho French Dip, taking the classic French dip and elevating its complexity by turning the beef broth into the flavors of pho.

DesiPDX, owned by coding wizard turned chef Deepak Saxena, specializes in "Local Fare, Indian Flair." Saxena combines classic Indian recipes with Western cooking techniques. The cart's name Desi doubles down on the cart's philosophy as it translates to something local or indigenous, as well as meaning someone from that part of the world living elsewhere. Dishes continually rotate throughout the seasons, focusing on organic and non-GMO ingredients whenever possible including their oils and spices; the menu is completely gluten free with paleo and vegan options. Crowds flock equally for

the red curry seitan and the tea-brined and fried chicken drumsticks. Whatever is chosen, a playful dance of complex spice blends will entertain the palate.

Newly renovated to provide covered seating for any season, the owner of the pod spares no expense to upgrade as it is in his best interest as owner of the Prost bar to curate some of the most popular carts in town and pair their top-notch bites with his top-notch German-style beers.

TIP

Wildly popular Matt's BBQ tends to sell out early, so make sure you go early or risk your favorite cut being sold out for the day.

THE WILLIAMS CRAWL

1. **XLB**, 4090 N. Williams Ave., (503) 841-5373, xlbpdx.com

2. **DOS HERMANOS**, 4082 N. Williams Ave., (971) 266-8348, doshermanosbakery.com

3. **JINJU PATISSERIE**, 4063 N. Williams Ave., (503) 828-7728, jinjupatisserie.com

4. **THE BOX SOCIAL**, 3971 N. Williams Ave., (503) 288-1111, bxsocial.com

5. **MF TASTY**, 3927 N. Williams Ave., (602) 740-8861, mftasty.com

6. **EEM**, 3808 N. Williams Ave., #127, (971) 295-1645, eemportland.com

7. **EAT: AN OYSTER BAR**, 3808 N. Williams Ave., #122, (503) 281-1222, eatoysterbar.com

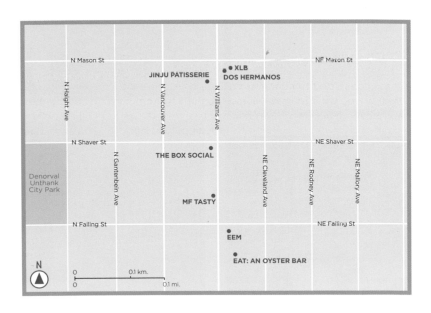

Williams

The hotspots on the short block

THE EVER-GROWING WILLIAMS DISTRICT is a rapidly changing neighborhood in North Portland, otherwise known as the fifth quadrant of Portland proper. As new buildings and spaces continue to be built, the district's rich history can still be seen, heard, tasted, and felt. Business owners are committed to honoring Williams's history while accepting change. Whether you want to grab yourself something from hands down the best happy hour deal in all of Portland, try inventive dishes from all-star chefs, or get some coffee and a bite to help bring you back to life after a hard night out, Williams District has got you covered.

1

XLB

This restaurant's name is shorthand for their signature dish, the Chinese comfort food *xiao long bao*, otherwise known as soup dumplings. Small handmade dumplings are filled, folded, and steamed to order and when bitten into burst with a flavorful soup. Do not be intimidated if it is your first time; every table has a helpful "how to" guide showing the proper way to eat this dish with instructions and pictures.

The small menu, which can be found in print or largely displayed on the wall with photos of each dish, offers about 12 items. There are a few focused *bao* (dumplings) that range in size from the petite *xiao long bao* to a larger *baozoi*, where three steam buns are filled with either a pork or mushroom and chive filling. Noodle dishes and plates meant for sharing come in small or large size, depending on how many people are sharing, but those who order the addictive Five-Spice Popcorn Chicken may want to order extra as this dish tends to leave guests fighting to get more than their share.

The Chinese influence flows into their signature cocktail the plum margarita; yeah, it's as good as it sounds. For the Wu-Tang Clan fan, the 36th Chamber of Oolong, comprised of vodka, oolong tea, coffee, and sweetened condensed milk, is almost a dessert in itself.

Happy hour is offered twice Sunday through Thursday, first from 5 to 6 p.m. and later in the evening from 9 to 10 p.m., as well as all day on Monday. Discounts on drinks and dumplings are featured, as well as a *bao* and beer combo that allows anyone to eat and drink like a king for less than $10.

Be sure to check the time before heading over, as they take a break between lunch and dinner service to allow all hands on deck to bulk up the handmade dumplings for the loyal neighborhood residents and visitors from all over.

2

DOS HERMANOS

Owned and operated by Gabriel and Josue Azcorra, **DOS HERMANOS** is part wholesale baker for local restaurant group Chefstable, and part local bakery. They make top-notch artisanal breads and rolls, and if you make it in time, you can catch some breakfast sandwiches and pastries before they sell out.

The English muffins are some of the best in the city, great for one of their breakfast sandwiches in-house or just stocking up for your place to toast the next morning.

TIP

If you happen to be staying at an Airbnb anywhere nearby, this is the place to stock up on stuff.

This Mexican bakery is also the most reliable spot in Portland proper to get a good *telera* roll, the standard bread used for all tortas. When the *hojaldra* is available, get it. This Yucatan specialty is a variety of pan dulce, with layers of dough stacked in between ingredients like ham, cheese and jalapeño before being baked and lightly dusted with sugar. Their focused beverage program offers coffees as well as specialty tea blends by T Project, a local studio that focuses on custom-made tea blends, utilizing the highest-quality, small producers. All blends are named after musical references from the 1960s and 1970s: pair a Ramble On with your biscuit, or if you are more of an Eagles fan, pair the Peaceful Easy Feeling with a fresh-made sandwich. While their rolls can be found throughout town in restaurants like Lardo and Sammich, Dos Hermanos gives customers access to restaurant-quality bread to enjoy at home.

3

JINJU PATISSERIE

JINJU, which is Korean for "pearl" or "treasure," is an apt name for this treasure of a dessert shop that newly opened on Williams. The duo behind this spot have some serious credentials. They met over a decade ago when master chocolatier Jin Caldwell met pastry chef extraordinaire Kyurim Lee while they both worked in Las Vegas. The caliber of establishments they collectively worked at would be enough to garner attention (Joel Robuchon, Aria, the Bellagio, the Wynn, and Green Valley Ranch to name a few), yet to add to their impressive resume Jin was also head of research and development for the world chocolate juggernaut the Mars Corporation and has been named one of the top 10 chocolatiers in North America. Their passion shows through

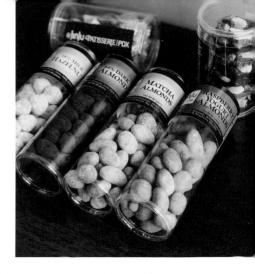

each sweet bite; they use the best, natural ingredients to showcase their skills and dedication to high standards.

Choose from an array of bonbons, ranging from such classics as dark chocolate to artfully decorated strawberry cheesecake, or the full-bodied flavor of green tea matcha. Do not pass on the pink lemonade or yuzu for light, interesting flavors that you would not expect when thinking of a bonbon. For a more substantial dessert, full-size creative offerings can be found in the display case to the left. Aside from the flavors, presentation is what makes this place stand out. For example, their layers of delicate chocolate cake are stacked in between light, velvet-like textured mousse, artfully placed and topped with abstract shapes of chocolate bark. The richest German chocolate cake can be found here, plated so beautifully you may hesitate to plunge your fork into it because you want to delay destroying a work of art.

Their offerings expand to some savory options. While all are excellent our favorite is the stuffed croissant with bacon and ham: because bacon! JinJu is a great way to experience top-tier luxury without the top-tier price tag. Portland was missing a patisserie on this level, but we had no idea until JinJu showed up.

TIP

There is a grab-and-go case for items that make great gifts for those with a sweet tooth in your life.

4

THE BOX SOCIAL

Your date night is going to be a great night if drinks are had at **THE BOX SOCIAL**, an intimate, laid back cocktail bar that has been slinging creative drinks and loosening inhibitions since 2011. Owners Eric and Shannon McQuilkin opened this romantic corner spot to much praise and a steady stream of loyal patrons. Their bartenders show a creative flair with twists on classics like the El Guapo, a margarita taken to another level by using the freshly squeezed lime half as a floating shot glass for mezcal that lets you decide when you want to take the night into overdrive.

Fun nibbles are available through their food menu, but the focus is on the cocktails. A main cocktail menu separates all the drinks by their base liquor. Each has a campy name, so if you're feeling like a vodka drink try the Ru Paul Sparkle Pony. One whiskey standout is the Young Man Blues

featuring Maker's Mark bourbon, brown sugar, lemon, bitters, and a float of Breakside Brewing IPA; strange as it may sound, this cocktail packs a punch while maintaining a balance that makes you want to order one after another. If the list does not call your name, there are a few other ways to get the party going. A bar that has a bottle selection stretching almost to the very tall ceiling offers a lot of choices. Have it neat or ask the cocktail wizards that work there to conjure up something to your liking.

If you're dragged here by your cocktail-loving buddy, they have a selection of bubbles, wines, and beers for those keeping it average. While this intimate spot subtly screams sexy time, make sure you take it home and not in their bathrooms; their sinks can't take it. Yes, they have a warning sign in the bathroom. Snap a photo of that or the flying cat during toilet time.

5 MF TASTY

After starting out as a pop-up restaurant in Phoenix in 2011, we turned our wandering concept into an elevated food cart that we refer to as a tiny restaurant. Unlike most Portland-area carts, which are housed together in groups known as pods, **MF TASTY** stands alone. There is seating for 28, including a shipping container turned into a dining room, aka the Tasty Box, which keeps you safe from any extreme elements. Guests can sip on rosé, mimosas, or local brews while soaking in the sunshine and listening to our curated playlist, heavy on the uncensored hip-hop.

Enjoy restaurant-quality dishes in a more relaxed setting without that restaurant price tag, but still on real plates. Our motto "Southwest Inspired, Portland Made" reflects our homage to familiar flavors from the 20 years we spent in Arizona, while utilizing Pacific Northwest ingredients as much as possible. Standout dishes include the POW! (Paella of da Week), made to order with rotating ingredients each week, and yes it includes *socarrat* (the distinctive crunch on grains of rice that have made contact with the paella pan)! The hangover killer, served all day, is our Almost Famous Brunch Burrito. It features two eggs scrambled, MF spiced potatoes, our Oaxacan cheese blend, pinto beans, and crema with choice of side salsa. Almost everything is made in-house, including the chorizo sausage, a popular addition to the burrito. Since building a bit of a cult following and with space being limited, specials can sell out quick, but no worries because everything is special and tasty AF. One example of this is the Biggie Mac, taking an American classic and giving it the chef treatment through butchering and grinding the beef to make our own burger blend fresh, the day of. We don't stop there; with details like scratch-made pickles and even microplaning the hard-boiled eggs into the secret sauce, this burger is next level.

We love to stay connected to the community through many events, including guest chef collaborations, special one-day menus, and shouting out other local small businesses to help nourish community rather than competition. People line up Tuesday evenings, as the regulars know this is the only night that the cart offers pressed to order blue corn tacos using

masa made by the local company Three Sisters Nixtamal that very morning. Nixtamalization is the ancient technique to get authentic tortillas, not something that a lot of places do because of how labor intensive it is. We think it is worth the extra cost, because you can taste the difference in each bite.

Those in the know follow the cart on social media so they can be the first to get that daily special before it sells out.

Have you ever had carne asada made with a high-quality cut like ribeye? You will here! All fancy meat aside, vegetarian, vegan, and gluten-free options are always available. We are happy to work with you to find something that works with your dietary restrictions; just be aware if there is a crowd behind you also waiting to order.

Regulars have found some secret menu hacks on their own, which keep things interesting for those that have gone through the whole menu. The menu may look small, but get creative and you will find a ton of options. We consciously source products from local companies doing things the right way. Friendly, personal, and genuine describes our brightly painted spot featuring a four-panel mural made by local artists Rather Severe. Good eats and sick beats: Let's face it, it's the opposite of basic.

6

EEM

Typically when you see a collaborative project from multiple well-known concepts the sum is never as good as the individual players; **EEM** is the exception to the rule. Guests get the best aspects of a trio of heavy hitters in Portland. Drinks from Eric Nelson, the founder of the wildly successful roaming bar Shipwreck pair nicely with the love child cuisine of Earl Ninsom's (Laangban, Pa Dee, Hat Yai) personal, soulful Thai flavors and pit master Matt Vicedomini's (Matt's BBQ) Texas-style barbecue techniques. Servings perfectly sized for a light meal alone, or to share with the whole table give groups the advantage of trying one of everything. Go wild while ordering because the prices won't have you worrying about breaking the bank.

One standout is the white curry with brisket burnt ends served over rice. Already deeply flavorful curry gets an additional layer of depth through the smoky essence that infuses itself from the brisket with each stir of the fork. The barbecue pork steak is a specialty cut bone-in pork shoulder, made as an homage to the specialty smoked pork steaks found at Texas barbecue joints. It jumps into another stratosphere of flavor when dipped in the *nahm prik noom* and *jaaw* dipping sauces.

As much as people come for the food, this is also a destination spot where drinks are not to be ignored. Creative, well balanced, and flavor forward, the cocktail menu offers something for everyone, including a few larger-format drinks that come in their own quirky, ceramic animals like a winking elephant or giant puffer fish. Eem's cocktail list rotates, but if you see the Nocturnal

Worker, try it—you'll thank us later. For those who do not drink but would still prefer a craft beverage over water, the mocktail list is extensive; it's hard to believe that this list has nearly as many options as the boozy drinks list. In the growing world of sober hospitality, this is an untapped market and they are getting in on the ground floor.

Be prepared to wait before you are seated. Put your name on the waitlist and stroll Williams while you wait.

Open and airy in the summertime, half of the walls are actually large garage-style doors that roll up creating a seamless transition from outside to in. You do not need to be from out of town to feel like you are on vacation when you are at EEM; the smoked meats and tropical drinks will have you feeling fine in no time.

7 EAT: AN OYSTER BAR

Specializing in cuisine south of the Mason-Dixon Line, **EAT: AN OYSTER BAR** not only offers Cajun and Southern American dishes but also an array of farm-direct oysters, rotating their offerings based on what is most fresh. When you go for oysters, do not expect cocktail sauce, but no worries, you will get a flavorful mignonette. Choose to have them by the dozen, half-dozen, or any mix and match combo of raw oyster varietals offered that day.

If you prefer more depth of flavor, as opposed to enjoying the unique subtleties of the raw offerings, choose from a handful of shooters or baked options each dancing to the rhythm of their own drum across your taste buds.

Huge po' boy sandwiches will feed two people, especially considering the abundant portion of fries that accompany them. We french fry aficionados highly praise them. Surprisingly light and crispy fried okra is a must and makes up for every bad version of this dish that exists in the world. Whether it is alligator or soft-shell crab, the specials board always has a surefire dish worth exploring.

Every Thursday, when ribs are the special, the smoker wafts a light perfume down Williams Avenue drawing in people from blocks away. The Cajun classic barbecue head-on shrimp served in a cast iron skillet with crusty bread is a go-to entree. Did you know that classic Cajun barbecue shrimp does not actually have barbecue sauce in it? It actually refers to how dark the final pan sauce looks. Enough with the fun facts, just order it!

Live bands for weekend brunch and Thursday evenings liven the place up with a group that has played almost as long as the Eat has been around, which is going on 10 years and counting!

THE ALBERTA ARTS DISTRICT CRAWL

1. **DEVIL'S DEN**, 1520 NE Alberta St., (503) 331-7119, every-day-wine -business.site

2. **TACOS PA'ELLA**, 1530 NE Alberta St., (503) 960-5858

3. **GUMBA**, 1533 NE Alberta St., (503) 975-5951, gumba-pdx.com

4. **MATTA**, 1533 NE Alberta St., (971) 258-2849, mattapdx.com

5. **LES CAVES**, 1717 NE Alberta St., (503) 206-6852, lescavespdx.com

6. **THE KNOCK BACK**, 2315 NE Alberta St., (503) 284-4090, theknockback.com

7. **BELLA PIZZA**, 2934 NE Alberta St., (503) 282-0600, bellapizzapdx .com

8. **URDANETA**, 3033 NE Alberta St., (503) 288-1990, urdanetapdx.com

Alberta Arts District

Stretch your legs, imagination, and waistband

A POPULAR TOURIST SPOT, THIS SEEMINGLY ENDLESS STRIP OF galleries, food carts, restaurants, and more can be found in Northeast Portland where for roughly 30 blocks, people can wander and explore while imbibing on a variety of options. One doesn't even have to walk more than 20 feet to travel from the flavors of France to Vietnam to Italy; shops and restaurants are stacked side by side, one after another. But wait! What's a person got to do to get a drink around these parts? Fret not, because there's a watering hole of every type. From craft cocktails, to subterranean wine bars that border on speakeasies, to dives, the Alberta Arts District has it. Huge murals from local artists can be found in almost any alleyway; some artists even have multiple pieces throughout the district. Regardless of which place you choose, half the fun is traveling to each spot and discovering treasures with every step.

1

DEVIL'S DEN

Billing itself as a low-key neighborhood wine shop, **DEVIL'S DEN** is the opposite of a pretentious wine bar. It is one of the few places serving alcohol that allows outside food (most places in Portland that are licensed to serve alcohol by law must offer food options and do not allow outside food). Neighbors, and those just visiting, grab some takeout from one of the many surrounding dining options and belly up to the bar, or one of the many tables, to enjoy a focused selection of wines that could be sold for far more than what they charge. Discounts are even given to those who support the surrounding food carts as their food choice. Generous pours put guests at ease that they are getting their money's worth.

Strolling the street with Fido? While there is no patio seating, Devil's Den allows well-behaved dogs inside with their owners, which is quite the bonus during the rainy season. The owner is almost always there tending bar, so the more you go, the more likely your wine preferences and dog's name will be remembered. The fair pricing extends to their bottle selection, which allows everyone to keep the party going by making sure you have a bottle or two to take home.

Be sure to check their events calendar, as they frequently host bands in addition to open mic nights, and even the occasional pizza pop-up will roll through.

2 TACOS PA'ELLA

Specializing in Mexican food from Jalisco, **TACO PA'ELLA** creates very affordable versions of a handful of tacos, burritos, chimichangas, and tortas. Friendly, simple, and honest is the best way to describe this cart. What you see is what you get, and what you get is simple, well-executed Mexican food for a steal of a price. Diners can take their choices to go or dine in the small covered area in front. Whatever you choose, add the pineapple-habañero salsa to create an addition that perfectly balances heat and acidity, bringing a new depth in taste to each bite. The secret to this sauce, which the owner will openly share with those who ask, is literally equal parts of pineapple and habañero! Nothing is over $5 on their menu, so those not looking to break the bank can feast to their heart's content. Perfect for a quick, small bite or feeding your whole crew for 20 bucks, Tacos Pa'ella has got you covered. Remember the phrase "don't judge a book by its cover," because this unassuming tin can has been a go-to spot for those in the know for tacos on Alberta Street for over five years.

TIP

The fish tacos are piled high with a mango slaw that has just the right acidity to cut through the grilled fish. One alone is filling, especially with the grilled jalapeño on the side.

3 GUMBA

The corner of Northeast 15th Avenue and Alberta Street houses a food cart pod with a few carts that rival full-service restaurants with their quality of food. That standout cart, one of the best in the city, is **GUMBA**. Owned by childhood friends Jesse Martinez and Robin Brassaw, this cart has been written up more than a disruptive child in school and for good reason; they make some of the best and most inventive pasta in Portland, all from scratch and for far less than one would pay in a brick and

mortar restaurant serving the same level of quality. The two pastas that have become the cart's gold standard are not to be missed; choose between silky pappardelle tossed in a rich beef short rib *sugo* that has layers of flavor or fresh tagliatelle served carbonara-style topped with sumac, lemon, fried shallots, garlic, and chili oil with their signature house-made burrata cheese . . . think fresh mozzarella but creamier. Inventive specials can range from utilizing items at the peak of their season to just a mental itch that Chef Jesse had to scratch. The love shines through with each carefully crafted dish, giving guests the feeling of dining at a refined Italian restaurant, if its kitchen decided to cook at a laid back patio party.

TIP

Gumba's daily-changing menu, as well as when their elusive and highly sought-after fried chicken sandwich is offered, can be found on social media.

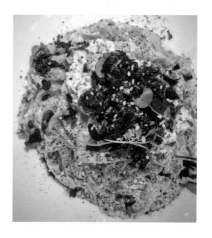

4 MATTA

MATTA is another distinct cart that happens to be next-door neighbors with Gumba, describing themselves as "Vietnamese Soulfood." Owners Richard and Sophia Le pay tribute to Richard's late mother through a small menu that changes daily and gives the feeling of family dinner. The Les take guests on a personal journey through reinterpreted versions of family recipes from the Le family's origins in Hue and Phan Rang, Vietnam, as well as a few childhood favorites. It is like being treated to a taste memory, a look into Richard's home life through each bite with the same welcoming hospitality that one would experience had they actually been invited to the Le household. Do not pass on their Pandan Donut with coconut milk glaze; you would not be the first to proclaim it is the best doughnut you have ever had.

While it may be hard to choose one place to dine within the pod, groups can order from all carts and share, tasting the flavors of three continents on one table. Unlike your standard food cart pod, which can feel sterile, this feels more like a fun, relaxed patio party; guests can take their food across the street to enjoy some adult beverages at Devil's Den wine bar.

5 LES CAVES

A fitting name for an underground wine bar, **LES CAVES** is exactly that. Finding it can be borderline speakeasy level. While walking down Alberta Street you will come across their A-frame, which is the only signage; go down that alley, down the stairs (be sure to admire the mural on your way down), and you've found the entrance. Housed in what was originally the boiler room for the original Victoria Theater at the turn of the 20th century, as well as a few churches post theater, Les Caves offers an intimate setting to get intellectual about wine.

Les Caves is the brainchild of the winemakers of Golden Cluster and Ovem Wines, doubling as their vineyard's tasting room, as well as showcasing their collection of wines from around the world. Their knowledge flows throughout the menu, focusing on organic and natural wines, rare vintages, a few beers, and even raw wines (a technique of wine similar to biodynamic, but nothing is added or removed during the winemaking process). Humorous in name, the Purple Drank is the house wine and a steal. Whether you are an industry insider, oenophile, or someone who knows jack about wine, there will be something interesting for you to try. Low ceilings, stone walls, and dim lighting all are inspired by the wine caves found throughout Europe.

Small bites are offered, but the most sought after bite is the grilled cheese. Simply made, the carefully selected ingredients give the feeling of a taste of childhood and elevated comfort simultaneously. What tastes like a buttery grilled cheese surprisingly contains no butter. Wisconsin Havarti and medium cheddar blend with the very hard to acquire Pirate Bread, which features a unique 48-hour fermented dough; those feeling luxurious can add thinly sliced *jamon serrano*, Spanish aged ham.

There is a private couch for two built into a cave within Les Caves that not only is the most sought after seat in the house, but gives those relaxing there an elevated view of all the action in the rest of the bar. After enjoying all the wine in your personal VIP area, be extra careful getting out as it's a bit of a jump down with a table right in front. You may have to ask them to move so you can leave without dropping into their laps.

6

THE KNOCK BACK

Debate can quickly ensue when asked to describe this local spot; the most apt way this bar has been painted is as a "divey cocktailery," a place where all pretenses are left at the door but the focus and expertise of a more refined drinking establishment comes through in their expansive liquor selection and delicious, thoughtful cocktails. This combination gives way to a best of both worlds scenario where a fun, laid back atmosphere offers great drinks, sans the epic ballad of how each drink came to be by your bartender.

Multiple covered patios offer plenty of expanded seating, one including a fire pit for brisk evenings and those who bring their dogs to hang out on the patio with them. It is the perfect place for you to stay cozy with a drink in hand and your pup by your side.

Every day happy hour offers a handful of drink discounts and specials, as well as an equal amount of bites, where nothing exceeds $7. For those feeling a little more adventurous than an Old Fashioned, and they do make a great one, a daily punch and daily slushee cocktail can be found. The extended cocktail list has something for almost everyone. From bourbon, to gin, to multiple year aged rum, each cocktail has the balance of a good twist on something familiar.

The sliders are excellent and each could be a signature sandwich at any restaurant. Offering nearly 12 different sliders or sandos, people can get exactly what they are feeling without breaking the bank. A heavy twist on

a light drinking snack is the Dirty Popcorn, a bowl of fresh-popped popcorn topped with bacon, spices, Romano cheese, herbs, and capers.

THE KNOCK BACK is a scene of its own and it is not unlikely that you will run into some of the service industry folk that took care of you elsewhere on Alberta; it has become quite the late-night industry place. The Knock Back earns its name as a place to make an evening out of or for a quick pop in to toss one back.

7 BELLA PIZZA

One of the longest-standing spots on Alberta, **BELLA PIZZA** has been slinging pies since 2001, focusing on hand-tossed, hearth-baked pizzas that have a nice balance of crispy and chewy dough. It's one of the few places around town that offers guests not only whole pizzas, but also many "by the slice" options. Without breaking the bank, people can come into this casual, inclusive environment to get a slice of old Portland: genuine pizza paired with a genuine love for Pearl Jam. While new construction has started to replace the old with the new, Bella brings guests to a pre-*Portlandia* era of Portland, something that is not as prevalent as it once was.

Brooklyn-born owner Linda Zumoff serves straight up East Coast pizza to

all who enter. When the weather is right, those who wish to still be connected to the hustle and bustle can dine outdoors on their cozy front patio, or if you prefer a spot more removed, indoor seating is plentiful as well as a back patio. They have multiple happy hour discounts, but for those over 21, a seven-day-a-week happy hour (4 to 6 p.m. and all day Monday and Wednesday) offers a steal of a deal where for $6, guests can choose between a slice of cheese or 'roni and a beverage, which includes beer, wine, or a well cocktail, perfect for the starving artist and thrifty diner alike. Vegan options are always available and gluten-free pizza is an option for whole pies.

Bella is not just around because they sling good pizza, but because they are connected to the community, from watching the neighborhood kids they feed turn into the neighborhood adults they feed, to giving back through their affiliations with local organizations.

TIP

Their house cocktails count for their slice and drink happy hour deal. So if you do the math that is only $3 for a paloma!

8

URDANETA

A picturesque boutique restaurant run by a couple who are clearly passionate about what they do, **URDANETA** is a chef-driven regional tapas restaurant that takes traditional flavors and showcases them through a modern interpretation. A classic salt cod is reinterpreted with olive oil candles that slowly melt and create flavor-infused dipping oil. Magically, as if the kitchen read your mind, a freshly baked mini loaf of bread appears at the perfect time to create a vehicle to soak up every last bit of this flavor bomb.

Chef Javier Canteras draws from a wealth of knowledge developed over his professional and personal experience growing up in northern Spain. Flavors from the most culinarily diverse region, Basque, are the focus of this tapas bar blending distinct Spanish flavors with the influence of its French border.

Their inventive and inviting food menu boasts a happy hour, known as Pinxto Hour referencing the classic tapas bar skewers, that offers multiple *pinxtos* and tapas from 5 to 6 p.m., Tuesday through Friday as well as drink specials. Their beverage program, which features an almost all

natural wine list and extensive sherry options, is not to be ignored. Their wine director, Jon Lawrence Joseph, has such a passion to bring unique offerings from small makers; guests often will be delighted by a bottle only to find out it was one of the last handful existing in the state!

Co-owner Jael Canteras is a welcoming beacon to guests as they enter, overseeing service and making sure the symphony of this small production flows seamlessly. The entire team, most of whom have been at the restaurant since it launched, have even taken team trips to Spain to research and learn through Javier's personal ties, deepening their connection to authentic Spanish cuisine.

On one trip the team ate so many of one variety of *pinxto*, they put it on the menu permanently, naming it Gilda. Gilda features *boquerones*, Basque *piparra* pepper, and anchovy-stuffed olive. Get it: Actually get all the *pinxtos*, which is a menu option if you find it too hard to pick a few, which you will.

THE FREMONT CRAWL

1. **ACADIA,** 1303 NE Fremont St., (503) 249-5001, acadiapdx.com

2. **HOLY GOAT SOCIAL CLUB,** 1501 NE Fremont St., (503) 282-0956

3. **LITTLE GRIDDLE,** 3520 NE 42nd Ave., (503) 752-7956

4. **BANG BANG/WONDERLY,** 4727 NE Fremont Ave., (503) 287-3846 and (503) 288-4500, bangbangpdx.com/wonderlypdx.com

5. **PIP'S ORIGINAL DOUGHNUTS & CHAI,** 4759 NE Fremont St., (503) 206-8692, pipsmobile.com

6. **PETER'S BAR & GRILL,** 5701 NE Fremont St., (503) 460-0544

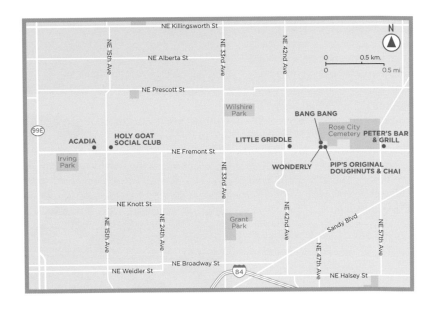

Fremont

Pass by the historic homes of the mom and pops that run the neighborhood hotspots

THIS PREDOMINANTLY RESIDENTIAL STREET STILL OFFERS A handful of food and beverage options worth exploring. Do you want to make it a bright, breakfast-filled morning, or do you want nighttime sexy lighting with small bites and thoughtful, tasty cocktails? If those two options do not sound appealing, you can throw down on some of the best wings in town at the neighborhood corner spot, and laugh to yourself knowing you are in on one of the best kept secrets in town, when it comes to the non-ironically rich culinary scene at Portland's dive bars. The choice is yours! Come with me, and you'll see a street of pure variation, filled with treats, plenty of sweets, and libations. We'll begin with a spin through breakfast creations. What we will see will defy expectations. Simply look around and view it, anything you want to eat, just remember to chew it. That's the range of variation that you will see on Fremont Street.

1

ACADIA

ACADIA is a relaxed bistro featuring cuisine from the Big Easy and a rich history to match those rich sauces. Chef-owner Seamus Foran cooked alongside former owner Adam Higgs as his sous chef for eight years before purchasing the spot in 2015 and taking over as head chef. Chef Seamus stays true to Acadia's original philosophy of honoring Louisiana by supporting Gulf Coast purveyors and serving domestic and wild-caught seafood from off the shores of Louisiana.

Tying in the marriage of the Pacific Northwest with this vision, local meats and produce are utilized, including a must-have pork chop. While foodies tend to overlook a pork chop on most menus for being "too safe," Acadia's version is not to be ignored. Local Carlton Farms supplies the succulent, behemoth chop that is served over boudin white corn grits, apples, black pepper-rosemary syrup, and pecans; big enough for two to share, this entree stands out among a menu of heavy hitters.

Packing a punch is their signature barbecue shrimp. Be sure to request an extra side of bread to mop up all that top-notch sauce. One example of their focus on Louisiana seafood can be seen in the striking presentation of fried soft-shell blue crab, a dish rarely found in Portland.

While the focus of operating hours leans toward dinnertime, on Wednesday Acadia opens their doors for lunch service, where the soft-shell crab makes a second appearance in one of the best po' boys to ever visit your taste buds.

Mondays are a day to expand your palette without blowing out your wallet; a handful of entrees are featured for $16, or opt for their three-course tasting menu with house salad and bread pudding for a cool $30. To find a spot that offers a three-course tasting menu for that price point, most have to wait for a special event like Portland Dining Month; here you can get that deal once a week.

2 HOLY GOAT SOCIAL CLUB

Got your mojo working? Travel down Fremont Street to a bar that should be considered an institution at this point and head on in to what was formerly known as Cafe Daddy Mojos, or Daddy Mojos, or just Mojos for short. Recently transitioned to new owners, the name changed to **HOLY GOAT SOCIAL CLUB** in September 2019, but the history has not left the building.

It's part dive, part sports bar, all neighborhood joint that has been around since before your time. The new captains behind the wheel, Leslie and Spyros, have been conscious of keeping the vibe from the good old days by keeping a lot of the old decor but giving this spot a small facelift. A curated selection of autographed headshots still adorns the wall, but now with a fresh coat of paint. New light fixtures brighten up the place, but with all the small new touches, the old-time regulars haven't abandoned ship.

Times may have changed, but the prices here have not changed much. A $7 breakfast gets you two eggs any style with a choice of two breakfast sides. Many Benedict options are topped with homemade hollandaise sauce along with almost another dozen breakfast options. The menu is extensive, and while you can't go wrong, we recommend the pub fare classic, the burger, mostly because it comes with their fresh-cut fries and as we know, fresh-cut fries are life. Be sure to opt for the half-pound over the

quarter-pound burger because those are served on a homemade bun, and trust us, you want the homemade bun.

Every other Friday evening folks clamor for their prime rib special that includes mashed potatoes, veggies, and a side salad with your choice of dressing for only $13.50, a steal of a deal as this could easily feed two people. If you do plan on splitting this special, you should get some fries, and actually throw on an order of the house-made onion rings while you're at it because those are pretty standout also. They come with a side of smoky ranch.

Every seat is a prime seat to watch the game with TVs that line every wall. If you feel like testing your luck, they have a video lottery section, and no need to stop at the convenience store because you can buy your lottery tickets here as well. This place has it all.

TIP

Although this is a full bar with restrictions on minors, all ages are allowed before 4 p.m.

3

LITTLE GRIDDLE

This pocket-sized brunch spot is freaking adorable and is easily found by the A-frame out front showing their mascot, co-owner Yossel Gyorgak's giant Boston terrier with a spatula in his mouth. This is the first time at bat as restaurateurs for owners Gyorgak and Judd Harris, who show bright enthusiasm for what they do and have experience from places like the cultishly followed Jam on Hawthorne. Upon opening one guest complained about a limited selection of hot sauces only to find owner Yossel quick to return after buying all types of hot sauces within a 3-mile radius to make sure there were more hot sauce options than anyone could ever want.

The bennies run aplenty from this tight menu that also features an array of biscuit sandwiches, grain bowls, and skillets. Do not skip the top-notch *shakshuka*, the classic Middle Eastern dish of eggs poached in a rich tomato sauce that has layers of flavor and is served with a side of crunchy, thick-cut grilled bread to dip or top with all that goodness, perfect for those who still like to play with their food a little. If you're feeling boozy try one of their drink specials like pineapple rum mimosas, or if you need caffeine to bring you back to the world of the living, Little Griddle has that strong cup of joe to get you in gear.

4

BANG BANG/WONDERLY

What happens when a bar with date-night vibes and Asian-inspired bites starts firing on all cylinders (Bang Bang)? Well in the case of owners Kate and Alex Wood, they take over the space next door and make another spot featuring a completely different menu with date-night vibes (Wonderly).

BANG BANG features a menu of Asian-inspired dishes with a focus on accommodating almost any dietary restriction; they take pride in how much their menu is gluten-, dairy- and peanut-free with vegan options to boot. They serve spirit-forward cocktails with a hint of restraint, meaning you can get a well-composed cocktail sans the history lesson from

some self-absorbed barkeep and can get straight into enjoying your drink. Case and point are the happy hour gin and tonics and Manhattans.

Multiple happy hours daily give you even more of a reason to give Bang Bang a visit; to make late night even sweeter there are 5 bonus items only available during this time including the Curry Fry Deluxe: Imagine if poutine took a semester off to go backpacking through Thailand. Fried chicken and garlic bits top a bowl of

coconut curry french fries with a soft egg and cilantro. Small details make the biggest differences; while most establishments carry Sriracha hot sauce, they make their own in-house and it is so good we make sure to buy a bottle of it every time we stop in. Rotating salads keep it seasonally fresh. Their pea leaf salad reads as if they were cleaning out the fridge and used those items to make a salad, but after you taste it you will wonder why more places do not have pea leaf salads on the menu.

If Asian inspiration does not inspire your appetite, their newest creation, **WONDERLY** next door, is a great alternative that showcases elevated bar food with a heavy focus on the cocktails. The sleek decor features dark wood tables and chairs, plenty of white and gold backdrops, velvet-covered

barstools, local art, mirrors, and plants. It is guaranteed to make you feel 100 percent cooler the moment you enter. Go for broke on their burger or save some cash by taking advantage of their happy hour food deals like fried cheese curds with hot honey, brussels sprouts doused in bacon vinaigrette, or American classics like shrimp cocktail and deviled eggs.

Like their sister restaurant Bang Bang, they offer two chances to hit up happy hour. Rinse it all down with a signature cocktail like the Oil Washed Alaska, featuring Oxley gin, olive oil, yellow chartreuse, orange bitters, and lemon oil. The unique Banhattan is another standout option because it has a brûléed banana as a garnish, and that alone is a reason to order this drink.

5

PIP'S ORIGINAL DOUGHNUTS & CHAI

By far the most Instagrammable of spots, **PIP'S** keeps it real, and they keep it simple, and for good reason. Fans from all over line up for the freshest mini doughnuts topped exactly as requested from their focused menu. From their open kitchen to their mini doughnut maker, watch their well-oiled machine keep the line moving; they move so seamlessly through everyone's orders while maintaining an upbeat vibe.

Seasonal doughnut fillings keep it fresh with options like Meyer lemon-pear butter, key lime pie with candied cranberry, or the ever popular banana custard. There is no wrong choice for your dough- nuts, but those in-the-know will do a quick scroll through the shop's social media to find out about the newest secret menu recipe. Online bragging rights will be yours as you amaze your friends with your insider knowledge, and who knows? Your pic may be so killer, they'll repost it!

Pip's is very actively engaged with their online community; just look up #communitynotcompetition and you'll find out the creator of Pip's is the creator of that hashtag. Although they have received many offers to expand, the owners choose to keep it "mom and pop" and con- tinue to be the only made-to-order doughnut shop in PDX.

While a lot of doughnut shops half-ass their coffee, Pip's serves killer cups of joe, and chai not to be messed with. Get a chai flight if you want to treat yourself to all that and then some, or just believe the hype on their drink called the Japanese Garden. Matcha blended with chai? Oh my! That's a hard yes.

No matter who you are, Pip's gives you an extra reason to cele- brate your birthday because you get a dozen b'day doughnuts for free! If you cannot make it on your actual birthday, you have up to seven business days after to get your free doughnut.

Open every day from 8 a.m. to 4 p.m., there is no bad day to go to Pip's; just give yourself a little extra time on the weekends.

TIP

They secretly stock the mini marshmallows found in hot chocolate packets as a topping. Pair that with a drizzle of chocolate and you've got yourself a s'mores-flavored doughnut.

6

PETER'S BAR & GRILL

This is the type of place you would drive by hundreds of times before stopping if you were not in the know. Part neighborhood spot, part dive bar, Peter's is a place to relax, watch the game on one of their many TVs, and get some of the best chicken wings in town, ironically across the street from a far more famous wing spot. Peter's wings give some of the bigger names in town a run for their money without the marketing budget.

Wings aside, choose from some classic bar bites, including quite the variety of specialty burgers that go beyond your frozen patty of sadness dive bar burger and execute at a level closer to a high-end bistro. While it is not written on the menu, request the Little League burger. Mini double patties are stacked in between an English muffin with . . . you know what? Don't worry about it because it is magic.

With options aplenty like the pool table often being open and available for free, and multiple video lotteries available in the back, as well as a patio and a front section that allows minors (during certain hours), there's just so much room for activities! Gambling, good food, games, and a variety of beers on tap under the same roof; this is the type of neighborhood bar everyone wishes was on their corner. If you're looking for a place with that real life Cheers vibe, Peter's is the spot for a genuine, affordable, fun time.

TIP

Even though it says Peter's on the sign, the owner's name is Tim. He may answer if you call him Pete, but everyone will know it's your first time.

THE EAST BURNSIDE CRAWL

1. **DELICIOUS DONUTS,** 12 SE Grand Ave., (503) 233-1833, deliciousdonutspdx.com

2. **CANARD,** 734 E. Burnside, (971) 279-2356, canardpdx.com

3. **DOUG FIR LOUNGE,** 830 E. Burnside, (503) 231-9663, dougfirlounge.com

4. **ATE-OH-ATE,** 2454 E. Burnside, (503) 445-6101, ate-oh-ate.com

5. **HOLMAN'S BAR & GRILL,** 15 SE 28th Ave., (503) 231-1093, holmanspdx.com

6. **CHEESE & CRACK SNACK SHOP,** 22 SE 28th Ave., (503) 206-7315, cheeseandcrack.com

7. **ANGEL FACE,** 14 NE 28th Ave., (503) 239-3804, angelfaceportland.com

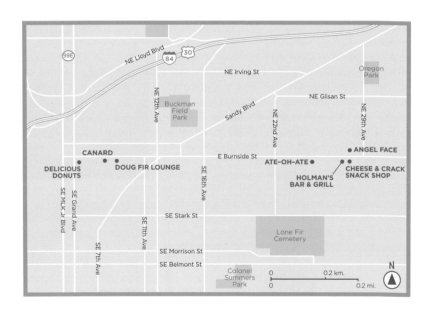

East Burnside

Where the cool kids in the biz set up shop

EAST BURNSIDE IS CHANGING AND STAYING THE SAME; it is the hub of east side transformation. New high rise buildings are housing new residents and changing skylines, but the area also houses the eateries of some of the most respected people in the food biz. Some are mainstays that have been around for a decade or more, and some are new projects from people who have already cut their teeth in Portland. Burnside marks the dividing line between North Portland and South Portland, but it brings the city together through these places. Get your morning sugar fix at one of the city's favorite doughnut shops or splurge on foie gras dumplings. Grab a shot, beer, and burger at a bar that was a speakeasy during the Prohibition era or hit up a new cocktail spot with no menu, just creative, skilled bartenders. These contradictions in concepts all have room to do their thing without stepping on each other's toes, which all in all makes for a great dance.

1 DELICIOUS DONUTS

Do you support small family-owned businesses? Do you love yourself some fried sugary pillows of goodness that pair well with a coffee? If you find yourself on East Burnside, then find your way over to **DELICIOUS DONUTS** where high school sweethearts turned husband-and-wife business owners Penny and Boun crank out some, like the name says, delicious donuts. Taking a family recipe and making it his own,

Boun has been making the donuts for over a decade now with Penny running the front, transferring her philosophy of "getting to know the patients" from her previous career of dental assistant into creating connections with the customers. Other connections can be found throughout the menu including a breakfast sandwich named after every family member.

The 3 Pigs Donut burger, which is two sausage patties, American cheese, hash browns, egg, and bacon sandwiched between two full-sized glazed donuts, is a delicious gut bomb named after three police officers who have been devout regulars for 14 years and counting. If available, order the elusive blueberry Old Fashioned; however there is always an interesting and very eye-catching Instagrammable option on the very top of the display case. Even the most stubborn donut snob will agree that this place is legit.

Know for sure you will be in the area? Call ahead and gain access to a few extra perks of their catering options only offered for next day orders, like large batches of donut holes or birthday donuts, which is exactly as it sounds: a birthday cake–sized donut customized as you like with house-made frostings and silly messages galore.

If you want inspiration for your next over the top custom donut, check their social media feed as there seems to be no message Penny won't get a kick out of writing. Often found on many of the city's "Best of" lists for donuts, Delicious Donuts shows that this little pup can not only run with the big dogs, but can teach them a trick or two while they're at it.

Get there early as they can sell out quickly. If you have a favorite, call ahead but make sure you show up as this small shop relies on every sale.

2 CANARD

If **CANARD**'s hours were a rap lyric it would be "all day, erry day" because it seems like there is no time this establishment from Portland restaurant royalty Gabriel Rucker and Andrew Fortang (Le Pigeon and Little Bird) is not open and getting shit done. The dining room and bar area give the feel of a Parisian bistro, simple yet chic. Iron shelving displays the liquors above the horseshoe-shaped bar area and the plateware is stacked high above the open kitchen where guests can see the action front and center.

The goals of the food and drink menus are to have as much fun as possible: mission accomplished! Dishes are priced between $6 and $20 and portioned to be the perfect size to share with a group, or make a light meal as a solo diner. Served anytime they are open, the Duck Stack is a Lamborghini-level rich version of a dish that only costs you Toyota Corolla-level dollars. Pancakes are smothered in rich duck gravy and topped with Tabasco onions and a sunny-side duck egg. If this is not rich enough, you can add seared foie gras to it!

The crispy calamari banh mi pays tribute to the classic setup with a healthy spread of velvety liver mousse and keeping the jalapeño garnish, but subbing in fried calamari and chili mayo to put the Canard stamp on it. People cannot stop talking about the steam burgers, and why would

they? They make you understand why Harold and Kumar just had to make it to that one place.

A smart way to start your meal is ordering one of the most talked about and photographed appetizers, Oeufs en Mayonnaise, aka a fancy AF deviled egg with trout roe, smoky bacon, garlic, and maple. Creativity does not stop in the kitchen.

The beverage menu has some unique cocktails and access to interesting wines, continuing on Le Pigeon and Little Bird's reputations for great bottle lists. Hard night out or looking for a snack with your drink? The Breakfast of Champions, a clever play on a gin martini, allows

you to add a fresh oyster to it, or should you want something a little meatier to sip on, have foie-infused bourbon in your Foie Turn. Are we sensing a pattern? French decadence flows through the menus; it's what you would imagine a concession stand to be if the carnival catered the opera.

A menu item never listed but always available is the Funfetti pancakes for the kid at heart. If all that is not enough fun for you, end your visit with a Funfetti dipped soft-serve cone; you may even luck out and get shaved truffles on it.

3

DOUG FIR LOUNGE

Attached to the wildly popular Jupiter Hotel, and often described as *The Jetsons* meets *Twin Peaks*, **DOUG FIR LOUNGE** has the feel of a modern log cabin. First timers' mouths drop and regulars are still dumbstruck over the design and vibe. You have many reasons to visit with its multiple bars, patio, restaurant, and music venue. With events and shows throughout the week, it is not out of the ordinary to realize you are having a cocktail next to the person performing downstairs, or a local celeb dropping in for a bite.

True story: While we were there checking out the new menu and not being discreet about staging our food for the best shot, we jokingly mentioned how this could be a *Portlandia* skit only to find Fred Armisen dining in the corner booth! Celebrities, they're just like us.

Let the good times roll any time of the day; they serve an all-day menu including happy hour. Whether you are flying solo or rolling deep with the whole crew, a space can be found to make sure everyone has a seat. A large dining room features comfy, spacious booths, and a long bar that looks as if one giant log was chainsawed in half runs all the way from the lounge to the restaurant. Opposite from the main dining room is the South Bar, which has some more intimately lit seating options to cozy up to your date and have a drink.

Peak hours can get busy, so reserving an area for birthday parties/special occasions assures everyone is comfortable for a successful night out. Walk through the lounge to an expansive patio that makes for great people-watching during the summer, as the nice

Check their daily calendar online for a full list of shows and events.

weather brings out the patio drinkers and occasional patio shows. The menu changes often, but you can always get a solid burger. Their vegan options are quite impressive; a group of us omnivores could not stop stealing bites off our vegan friends' plates. Drinks are reasonably priced, and given the elaborate, aesthetically pleasing atmosphere, you would imagine they charge a lot more than they do.

With shows galore, a menu that practically never stops, and tons of unique and inviting areas to make your own, the Doug Fir Lounge is perfect for a quick stop, or to make an evening out of.

4 ATE-OH-ATE

Owners Ben Dyer, Jason Owens, and David Kreifels use high-quality ingredients and island flavors to make them stand out from many of the other Hawaiian eateries in town. With Oregon having the highest population of Hawaiians outside of Hawaii, that is no easy feat. The counter service at **ATE-OH-ATE** offers a variety of classic plate lunches, sandwiches, and sides: all the island flavors for less than $13 a plate.

Those in the know will pounce on the fantastic happy hour deals offered daily from 4 to 6 p.m. Classic drinks are reasonably priced all day, but their happy hour Mai Tai packs a serious punch for only $7. You'll feel that punch if you decide to finish a second one. And then you're done; they literally will not sell you a third.

Food standouts from happy hour include a $6 cheeseburger that rumor has it is sourced from the same high-quality beef at Laurelhurst Market, a high-end steakhouse owned by some of those behind Ate-Oh-Ate. Spam musubi tempura takes us back to trips to the Aloha State with every bite, and the $3 fried rice is enough to make a meal in itself. You know what? Might as well just order the whole happy hour menu, because if you get one of everything, it is only around $30 for all 10 food items!

Larger groups can be sat easily in one of their bigger booths, and kids are welcome at all hours. Ate-Oh-Ate gives you the island experience without the flight.

5

HOLMAN'S BAR & GRILL

Mark Twain once said, "Too much of anything is bad, but too much good whiskey is barely enough." If that is the case, consider **HOLMAN'S** whiskey club barely enough of a selection of the good stuff. To be clear, this bar serves all sorts of alcohol, but what catches your eye front and center is the display for the whiskey club, a whiskey drinking program. Those who complete it get their names engraved on a brass plate, and their glory lives on hung up behind the bar, becoming part of the bar's history. If you visit on a Wednesday you can get whiskey at a discount, which can be helpful if you are trying to join the club.

Transforming throughout its existence, Holman's Bar & Grill started

as a tiny lunch counter that (legend has it) was a bootlegger's saloon during the Prohibition era. After the 1933 repeal it was renamed the "Hello Inn." The current owners, BC and Judy, bought the place in the 1970s and expanded from less than a dozen seats to the multiroom bar that it is today. Each room has its own story of what it used to be. The north dining room was part of a neighborhood drugstore; the game room that now houses a pool table, darts, and arcade games was once a bicycle and lawn-mower repair shop; the back garden patio was converted from an old used appliance graveyard.

Open seven days a week from 8 a.m. to 2:30 a.m., their all-day menu offers breakfast, lunch, and dinner choices, but make sure you get the scratch-made fries. As two french fry aficionados, we can attest to the high-quality spuds. Do not skip the fries! You know what goes great with said fries? Their burgers. Get a slider or get a regular-sized one.

Weekend mornings are the time to customize your hangover cure with Portland's original Bloody Mary bar, where drinkers can choose from over 100 mixes, hot sauces, and fresh garnishes.

While prices are super reasonable, you may even get your meal on the house if you win big on Holman's famous "Meal Wheel." Each diner has an opportunity to spin the wheel, and if you match up the two red arrows, your food is free!

There have been over 17,000 winners of the Holman's "Meal Wheel," resulting in over 17,000 free meals!

6

CHEESE & CRACK SNACK SHOP

Another food cart turned brick and mortar restaurant, **CHEESE & CRACK** specializes in two things, but what is the crack? According to owners William Steuernagel and Nathan Hall, it's just everything that is not cheese! Guests can choose from a handful of plates that all come with house-made savory oatmeal cookies, baguette, olives, cornichons, dijon, honey, chocolate ganache, and house-made rustic butter crackers. If you want it more customized, there are many add-ons available, ranging from an extra type of cheese to a mini order of French onion soup when in season.

Those who just want it all should order the Sample Plate Deluxe where you can get all the cured meats and cheeses on one gorgeous board that will be equal parts party in your mouth and the envy of all your social media followers. Not to sound whack, but the crack is where it's at.

Save room for dessert because their addictively good vanilla soft-serve deserves all the hype thrown its way. This is the perfect example of something simply done, perfectly. To jazz it up choose to give a light dusting of matcha, beet, strawberry dust, or the oh-so-extra chocolate ganache with espresso dust sprinkles. Both sundae options, the Cheese & Crack Sundae or the Mud Sundae take that delicious soft-serve base and add a bunch of crazy flavorful layers, perfect for those who want "all the things" in one thoughtfully built dessert. Our favorite is the Cheese & Crack Sundae, which features chocolate ganache, cinnamon butter cracker crumble, and vanilla soft-serve topped with a house-made brûléed marshmallow. It may sound like a sundae that you have had before, but this one is far better.

Fun drink options are available, whether you are imbibing or not; their delicious frozé is just as refreshing as their lemonade spritzer. Open every day, Cheese & Crack Snack Shop offers savory and sweet treats to anyone wanting to see why simple can be so much more.

7 ANGEL FACE

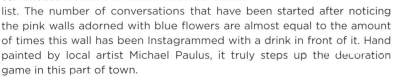

Can you just not decide what to drink? Maybe you're particular to a certain spirit or flavor profile but want to have something new, but you just can't put your finger on it. The magicians pouring up the concoctions at **ANGEL FACE** can guide you in the right direction, because there is no cocktail menu. After a few questions from the staff, your drinks are concocted to order leaving you feeling satisfied and curious as to how they manage to exceed your expectations every damn time.

Those who want to know what is in their cup can choose from the shoebox-sized bar's wine list. The number of conversations that have been started after noticing the pink walls adorned with blue flowers are almost equal to the amount of times this wall has been Instagrammed with a drink in front of it. Hand painted by local artist Michael Paulus, it truly steps up the decoration game in this part of town.

This refined 20-seater is perfect for a small group or date, or for any crowd with an appreciation for good drinks, willing to put their faith in the bartenders to do what they do best. While Angel Face is not a budget bar experience, it still is fairly affordable with cocktails typically ranging from $7 to $9 and food $10 to $17. Food is on the snacky end, but the flavors are thoughtfully stacked to create maximum impact.

CENTRAL EAST SIDE CRAWL

1. **REVELRY**, 210 SE MLK Blvd, (971) 339-3693, revelrypdx.com

2. **SCOTCH LODGE**, 215 SE 9th Ave Ste 102, (503) 208-2039, scotchlodge.com

3. **COOPERS HALL**, 404 SE 6th Ave, (503) 719-7000, coopershall.com

4. **DANWEI CANTING**, 803 SE Stark St, (503) 236-6050, danweicanting .com

5. **WILD NORTH**, 930 SE Oak St, (971) 808-1202, wildnorthpdx.com

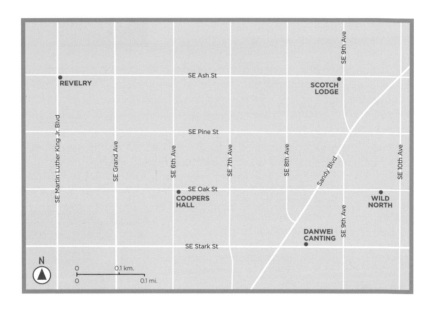

Central Eastside

Industrial on the outside,
warm and friendly on the inside

TO THE UNTRAINED EYE, THE CENTRAL EASTSIDE SECTION of Portland can seem like a lot of commercial buildings and warehouses—a part of town not meant for leisurely strolls. Look a little closer and you will find some great spots to pop in for a bite and a drink with even better happy hours! Because let's face it, everything tastes better when you get a deal on it. Pop bottles while sitting around the corner from the barrels that contain the next vintage at Coopers Hall. Beijing-style home cooking can be found blocks away from banging hip-hop and shareable kimchi pancakes.

1

REVELRY

With their first venture outside of Seattle, chefs Rachel Yang and Seif Chirchi give Portland a taste of Seattle without the drive, but with even later hours and more gusto. Asian eats with hip-hop beats are what is served at **REVELRY**, and unless you are a die-hard country fan, this is the spot to get the party started or keep it going. Street art murals canvas the walls, and one does not have to look too hard to find the live DJ on Friday and Saturday nights spinning tunes to keep the crowd upbeat and the party vibe alive. The fun flows from the atmosphere to the food and beverages. Guests can enjoy a selection of sochu, sake, beers, and wines, but we recommend

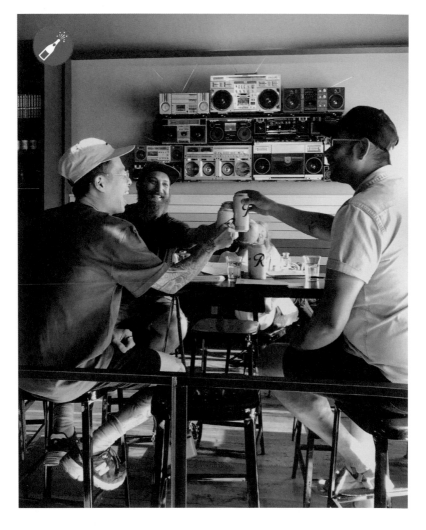

letting the barkeeps do their thing and make a signature cocktail for you. The food is on point, a distinct highlight being Mrs Yang's spicy fried chicken topped with peanut brittle—a great balance of heat and sweet. Get it for an even better deal on Tuesday evening when you can grab a petite order and a Rainier tallboy for only five bucks. If any place should be charging fifty dollars a bucket, it should be this place; good thing they are giving Portland a price break! Multiple happy hours give you multiple chances to save big while enjoying drool-worthy bites and libations; happy hour is offered daily from 4 to 6 p.m., as well as from 10 p.m. to midnight Fridays and Saturdays. Whatever time you go, Revelry will be ready with those flavor fireworks.

2 SCOTCH LODGE

We love scotch. Scotchy, scotchy scotch. Get in our belly. If you happen to share this trait with Ron Burgundy, **SCOTCH LODGE** will be your happy place. *Anchorman* references aside, Scotch Lodge is a cocktail bar for whiskey lovers with a modern French menu of fun snacks to complement those drinks. The bar is located underground, so you will find yourself following the signs to the basement of the building it is housed in, leading you to a place that feels like a secret. Once inside you'll find a stark contrast to the bare hallways that led you inside; warm low lighting highlights the beautifully crafted bar and intimate booths that line the walls.

While the term "craft cocktails" has been thrown around so much it almost lacks the distinction it once held, these cocktails have been carefully crafted to stand out far above the standard these days. The Burnt Orange Sherry Cobbler makes us wish dessert could always be this good, with a combo of Japanese whiskey, sherry, burnt orange, and a dash of sugar. The food matches these high standards with standouts such as a soft-shell crab sandwich on Japanese milk bread with hot mustard kewpie (a type of mayo) and kimchi remoulade (think fancy thousand island). Crudo and at least one pasta stay on the menu to give this intimate space a little something for everyone. Don't pass on the pomme frites, which are great for sharing, but after tasting the dill pickle spice on these spuds that continues to flavor the sour cream dip the more you dunk, you may be telling your dining companions to order their own!

Knowledgeable, friendly staff keep the party going while answering all your questions. You can tell they are happy to be there and genuinely excited to be sharing their unique offerings.

3

COOPERS HALL

COOPERS HALL resides in a unique structure built in the mid-20th century, a former auto body shop with no confines between the winery and tap room. The spacious environment invites guests to get closer to all aspects of the wine-making experience from grape to bottle. Sip some of the wines available on tap and take a bottle home that is freshly poured and capped to order with one of their reusable growlers. Coopers Hall

is perfect for a night out drinking, dinner with friends, or large events and private parties. Locally sourced, sustainable, and seasonal ingredients aren't just buzzwords here; they are part of the daily routine. The food, which draws from French and Alsatian influences, maintains excellent quality while celebrating local farms.

4

DANWEI CANTING

Boasting that they bring the best of China to Portland, **DANWEI CANTING** carries on the tradition of Beijing street food in a central hub for all the people. The name is derived from central dining halls found in China where work units would break and recharge during their shifts; because the units came from all over, the chefs learned regional specialties to give the roving groups a taste of home. While the counter service model can be a little daunting for those who have not tried this style of cuisine, the helpful staff and menu with large colorful photos of each

dish make it easy to choose what new tastes your palate gets to experience. Chili-heads and those who prefer milder dishes alike will find something to make them happy. Wash it all down with a bottle of Tsing Tsao or one of their specialty cocktails.

Much like the original concept, Danwei Canting is a place for people from all over to get together and enjoy something royal in flavor at a price point that any worker can afford. The tofu, which they get from Ota Tofu factory directly across the street, couldn't be any fresher! If anyone asks if you want some nuts in your mouth here, say yes because their black vinegar peanuts are where it's at. You really can't go wrong no matter what you choose, from their Szechuan peppercorn street fries to any of their wide wheat noodle dishes. This is one of those rare spots where there are no bad choices. Open windows show all the action on Sandy Boulevard and the patio.

5

WILD NORTH

Terms like "nose to tail eating," "hyper-seasonal," and "zero waste" tend to be reserved for restaurants, but at the **WILD NORTH** cart they feel right at home. Partners in business and life, Brandon and Amelia Hughes combine their love of the great outdoors with rustic cooking techniques—everything comes out of their single wood-fired oven. Bread bowls for seasonal soups are baked daily using a family sourdough starter that is over

fifty years old! The menu highlights fresh, seasonal, whole-ingredient dishes in which everything finds a home to minimize waste and maximize flavor.

When they aren't tapping local farmers' bounty for their creations, Brandon and Amelia garden or forage the ingredients themselves. Mondays are the only night to get in on one of their sourdough pizzas, which they offer from 6 to 9 p.m. or until sold out, which easily can happen when the patio is hopping. Personal touches go beyond their connection to ingredients with a spice rub for sale based on Amelia's father's signature family mix, aka Paul's Almost Famous spice rub, which makes a great gIft for the grill master in your life. You can taste every bit of the Pacific Northwest, as every ingredient is sourced within 100 miles of Portland.

While we don't recommend wandering far while they make your order, they will give you an electronic buzzer to let you know when your food is ready. Walk 100 feet away to the neighboring Base Camp Brewing Company for a pint or flight while the best of the Pacific Northwest is made to order for you.

THE BONUS BEER CRAWL

1. **WAYFINDER BEER**, 304 SE 2nd Ave., (503) 718-2337, wayfinder.beer

2. **LOYAL LEGION**, 710 SE 6th Ave., (503) 235-8272, loyallegionpdx.com

3. **MODERN TIMES BEER**, 630 SE Belmont St., (503) 420-0799, moderntimesbeer.com

4. **CASCADE BREWING BARREL HOUSE**, 939 SE Belmont St., (503) 265-8603, cascadebrewingbarrelhouse.com

5. **BASE CAMP BREWING COMPANY**, 930 SE Oak St., (503) 477-7479, basecampbrewingco.com

Bonus Crawl!

Beer: There are just so many breweries

PORTLAND CURRENTLY RANKS EIGHTH IN CITIES THAT HAVE THE most breweries per capita in the United States, so you would be doing yourself a disservice if you didn't try a few different pints in the area. There are so many to choose from: How do you tell which one is worth going to? It's a trick question because they all pour some high-quality suds; some just happen to be better than others. While you can always order something local at practically every place that you go, sometimes it is best to go to the source. Here is a list of some that happen to be around "Brewery Row" where a stretch of breweries have laid roots to start brewing those hops. Hop from one to the next and find your next favorite.

1

WAYFINDER BEER

You know you are in for a fun time when the establishment's motto is "Maybe Partying Will Help." **WAYFINDER BEER** will lead you there with solid beers and food that keep up the reputation of cofounders Charlie Devereux (Double Mountain Brewery in Hood River), Matthew Jacobsen (Sizzle Pie), and Rodney Muirhead (Podnah's Pit and La Taq). Whether it is the gigantic 2000-square-foot deck with fire pit or the 110-seat interior, there is surely a spot for you and your crew to get comfy and follow that company motto.

The interior is broken up into a few rooms. Guests enter and are immediately in front of the taps that serve all those delicious lagers and ales brewed onsite, with large tables and booths spaced throughout. Go to the left and find even more seating with the 10-barrel setup in full view along with the open kitchen.

Try the crisp Hell lagerbier and you will see why they were given a slew of awards for those suds. As it is the Pacific Northwest, there are plenty of IPAs at your disposal. With their tap list rotating depending on what they are brewing, guests can check their frequently updated website to see what they are pouring that day, and even what is available to take home. We are not just talking about sixpacks; should you choose, you can buy full kegs to go!

Basic bar snacks level up with not to be missed carne asada fries that feature wagyu skirt steak, avocado salsa, red onion, cheese, and crema that have us drooling before they hit the table. Rodney's barbecue chops get shown in the Black Lodge Sandwich: smoked prime rib, beer cheese, peppers, and onions are all stuffed in a French roll that will have any-one swearing off cheesesteaks from anywhere else. Off the beaten path, amongst the industrial warehouses, Wayfinder is a gem hidden in plain sight; you just have to find the way.

2 LOYAL LEGION

While Portland may have the eighth most breweries per capita than anywhere else, few places try to offer a taste of them all. **LOYAL LEGION** is a central beer hall trying to showcase as many as they can with 99 local beers on tap. If that isn't enough, be extra and request their cellared beer list.

They are open every day, practically all day and night, so there is never a time when you or a huge group can't roll in to taste one of the biggest local tap lists around. The inside decor is a sleek, minimalist look with leather booths bordering practically every edge of the room, ranging in sizes from a two-top to large booths for bigger groups looking to have their own space to party. Center stage is the grand wrap-around bar housing a massive tap system. Order a pint of Oregon brew or tasting flight to see what your new favorite local beer may be.

Are you that person in the group that just doesn't do beer, but everyone else decided to go to a beer hall? Save everyone the headache of how there is just nothing there for you because Loyal Legion has an extensive and delicious cocktail program with an entire page dedicated to the Old Fashioned, offering 10 varieties of the classic that each could be its own new classic.

Bites offered revolve around classic bar food with plenty of vegan options. The standout is their vegan take on buffalo wings using cauliflower; drenched in buffalo sauce,

yet somehow still crispy, this is an option so good you'll want it whether you eat meat or not. Everything goes great washed down with a glass of, you guessed it, beer.

Offering a daily four-hour happy hour, from 2 to 6 p.m., and late-night menu after 10 p.m., there are so many opportunities to snag a deal. If you want to go brewery hopping but would prefer to skip the tour bus, go to Loyal Legion and taste all of Oregon without leaving your stool.

3 MODERN TIMES BEER

Otherwise known as the Belmont Fermentorium, this is the latest outpost of San Diego's Modern Times Brewing. **MODERN TIMES** puts their spin on the former Commons Brewing space with minimalist decor with bright splashes of color in the form of colored yarn spun into wall-size designs that clearly took a long time to make. Find '90s-era nostalgia when you roam the hall with beer in hand. Interactive toy displays are there for you to play with. Sip on a coffee stout and watch a California Raisin fight a Teenage Mutant Ninja Turtle. Mosaic tiles made out of old floppy discs line the wall behind the taps and front of the bar. How's that for adaptive reuse!

A variety of suds are offered, from hazy IPAs to standout sours, some brewed onsite and some from their California locations. The menu is completely vegan with a burger from Beyond Meat and vegan delights so good you will not even realize that they lack dairy. Tables are also available upstairs.

With eye-catching designs around the brewery, as well as their cans, there are plenty of backdrops worthy of your next social media post. If you are rolling in on a party bus with a group of 15 or more people, they do request that you reach out in advance as this place always seems to be packed.

4 CASCADE BREWING BARREL HOUSE

If you are into sour beers, drop what you are doing and get yourself over to **CASCADE BREWING BARREL HOUSE**, which not only offers a menu that is predominantly sours but also boasts being the innovator that brought the Northwest Sour Ale. If you only drink the type of beer that is advertised during *Monday Night Football*, keep walking because this is the barrel house that keeps it interesting, with barrels sourced from Kentucky bourbons and Northwest wines that add another level of complexity. Twenty-eight rotating taps keep the party in your mouth going. Their website is always up to date to keep you in the know about what is being poured at the moment, with notes about which beers are available canned, bottled, and in growler form for you to take with you for later. Older vintages are bottled and available for purchase, letting the drinker compare different vintages of the same beer. Sit on the expansive covered patio and people watch during any weather and see who is also stumbling down Belmont  on their own beer crawl. They say learning is fun, and no one can argue with that when it comes to tasting interesting beers. Catch a buzz while expanding your knowledge of some tart and tasty sours.

5 BASE CAMP BREWING COMPANY

When mountaineering, base camp is what your group hikes do to set up shop, rest, and check their gear before hitting the hard stuff ahead. **BASE CAMP BREWING COMPANY** offers something similar: a place to take a load off and gear up on some small-batch brews with you guessed it, a mountain climbing theme. Although you may need to ascend a flight of steps to get into the tasting room and bar, to get this journey going the only gear you will need is a shirt and shoes. Soaring high ceilings and spaced-out high-tops give you and your party plenty of room to traverse the menu, ranging from lighter lagers to heavier stouts, some of which even come with a mini brûléed marshmallow on top!

Offering a unique twist on the mandatory food menu required at establishments serving booze, Base Camp outsources the food to some experts in the food cart game by hosting them on their outdoor patio, which in winter weather is covered by a tent that could fit a small mountain range and offers plenty of refuge from the harsher winter elements. The carts sometimes rotate to keep the clientele engaged with variety, so if you don't happen to find Wild North here, there is sure to be another great dining option to complement your drink.

In addition to all these offerings, Base Camp has a retail outfit ready for you to refill your growler or take a sixpack of your favorite home with you. While eventually you have to pack up your gear and keep the journey moving, Base Camp is a perfect spot to rest, refuel, and recharge before continuing your ascent to great food and drinks.

THE HAWTHORNE CRAWL

1. **SAPPHIRE HOTEL, 5008 SE Hawthorne Blvd., (503) 232-6333, thesapphirehotel.com

2. **NICK'S FAMOUS CONEY ISLAND, 3746 SE Hawthorne Blvd., (503) 235-3008, nicksfamousconeys.com

3. **PORTLAND CIDER HOUSE, 3638 SE Hawthorne Blvd., portlandcider.com

4. **BABY BLUE WOOD FIRED PIZZA, 3207 SE Hawthorne Blvd., babybluepizza.com

5. **TOV COFFEE & TEA, 3207 SE Hawthorne Blvd., (541) 908-2555, tovcoffee.com

6. **CUBO, 3106 SE Hawthorne Blvd., (971) 544-7801, cuboportland.com

7. **OK OMENS, 1758 SE Hawthorne Blvd., (503) 231-9959, okomens.com

8. **BARK CITY BBQ, 1080 SE Madison St., (971) 227-9707, barkbbq.com

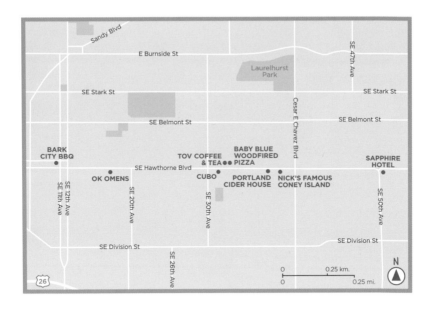

Hawthorne

Portland's most eclectic street

KNOWN FOR ITS ECLECTIC MIX AND BOHEMIAN VIBE, the dream of the '90s has not died on Hawthorne. Drinks from a hotel with no rooms make for a great date night before heading to some dining destinations from well-seasoned chefs that share the block with casual drop-in spots. With all the quirky gift shops, bookstores, and resale boutiques that line Hawthorne, you're going to need a few breaks for refueling, and this street has options galore. It has found a symbiosis of charming dive bars, vintage institutions, and newer places that deliver the goods. The east side location of the famous bookstore Powell's sits on this oh so popular street. You may see the locals hauling their bags of clothes to consign at the many resale shops within walking distance of each other. People-watching is prime, so if you can snag a patio seat go for it and enjoy the show. Coney Island–style hot dogs are down the road from casual Cuban food, and after you start feeling the meat sweats, you can grab a pick-me-up Egyptian coffee from inside a double-decker bus. Once you feel recharged you can come down from the top patio of that bus and hit the pavement for more flavor fireworks.

1

SAPPHIRE HOTEL

In what was once the lobby of a brothel at the turn of the 20th century, **SAPPHIRE HOTEL** is still a place people go to grab a cocktail and maybe meet someone to have a good time with. But nowadays you can't rent rooms by the hour upstairs as they are now private apartments and prostitution is no longer on the menu. While the social interactions may differ, the lobby still makes for a great place to gather with a group or just your date to enjoy some creative drinks in a dimly lit, romantic cocktail bar. Their drink menu shows the staff's clever and fun energy, divided into sections like "What We Drink" featuring drinks that are named after the staff member that enjoys that libation in their off hours.

If you are stuck on what to order, there is always the "Dealer's Choice" where you let them shake up something magical. Do you find some of these fancy brands and ingredients confusing or unfamiliar? While some cocktail bars make you feel less than for not knowing, Sapphire Hotel has proactively placed a glossary at the back of their menu to help educate their guests, leaving you at ease to actually know what you ordered.

Food errs on the snack-heavy side, with appetizers aplenty and meant to share. A handful of items including simple pastas, vegetarian and meat-based burgers, as well as a few entrees make for a tight food menu that complements the thoughtfully created concoctions.

Portland loves its brunch, and Sapphire Hotel tapped popular chef Risa Lichtman of Le Page Food & Drinks to create a menu of seasonal bangers. While brunch is only offered on the weekends, they are open every night, so any night is the right night to check in to the Sapphire Hotel.

TIP

Despite the name, it is not an actual hotel. Bring your appetite, but not your baggage!

2

NICK'S FAMOUS CONEY ISLAND

Started in 1953 with the single goal of making a damn good Coney dog (the Coney Island name for a chili-covered hot dog), **NICK'S FAMOUS CONEY ISLAND** has succeeded in that goal and turned itself into a neighborhood institution along the way. As the street continues to change with Portland, this spot is a welcome refuge to all, free of any glitz or glam, but chock-full of history and super affordable everything. Not everything is smothered in chili, but you'll want to try theirs because they've made a version that is clearly worth writing about! While it may seem on the divey

side, there are local microbrews on tap and the hot dogs are now from local butchers. Who can complain when you keep all the good parts of an old-school hot dog joint and step up the quality of ingredients? If the local IPA sounds too fancy to wash down that chili dog or burger, there's always some High Life available for anyone that wants to keep it more low key. Old-school cool with new-school quality is the type of combo anyone can get behind.

Generations of people call this place their *Cheers* as it has been going strong for over 60 years, so it is not uncommon to find generations of the same family who have all had their drunken 21st here, as well as a lot of industry peeps throwing back shots after a shift. Drop down onto one of the original barstools, slide into a super comfy booth, or order up and hit the game room in the back; anywhere you get cozy you will get solid service.

3 PORTLAND CIDER HOUSE

Portland Cider House owner Linda Parrish yearned for a style of cider she had enjoyed during her time in England. She and her husband Jeff started with closet cider and eventually formed a full-on legit company. Amongst the vintage shops and movie theaters with historic features, this tasting room has all the modern amenities one could ask for. Walk past over a dozen large high-top tables to the bar where large flat-screen TVs showcase the current offerings. The clean, minimalist decoration of all wood everywhere seems to be the style. Board games are available for those who want to make their tasting last a little longer or wait out the rain. Trivial Pursuit cards are on each table to help jumpstart a conversation with your drinking buddies should there be a lull.

While this cider house offers a substantial number of sweet and fruit-forward ciders, novice and more experienced cider drinkers can still commingle here. You will find complex options with their reserve list of barrel-aged ciders. Pick a pint, a flight, or even take it to go with their growlers and sixpack options. Food is smartly divided into how you are feeling, so if you just want a light snack choose something from the "Peckish" section like their hummus plate or a basket of tots; and if you are straight up hangry choose a sandwich from their "Famished" section. You will likely take your out of town guests to Hawthorne, so why not pop in and give them a taste of some of the cider Portland has to offer?

4

BABY BLUE WOOD FIRED PIZZA

After changing to a plant-based diet, Odie O'Connor found that he could not find a vegan pizza to satisfy his most-missed omnivore food, so he struck out to make one himself. He picked up a copy of local hero Ken Forkish's cookbook, *Flour Water*

Salt Yeast, and got to practicing. What started as positive feedback at backyard hangouts encouraged owner Odie to take the plunge into the Portland pizza game, filling a void left by a lack of crave-worthy plant-based pizza options around town. After learning from Gracie's APizza and running as a pop-up, **BABY BLUE WOOD FIRED PIZZA** found a permanent home on SE Hawthorne in the form of a food cart.

Each pie begins with a sourdough starter that originated from the chef's former employer and mentor Craig of Gracie's. While vegans rejoice and sing the praises of his dough, which blends a balance of crispy outside giving way to the right amount of chew inside, meat eaters and vegans alike are satiated and satisfied. Flavorful plant-based substitutions like faux pepperoni and pork belly taste as close to the real thing as possible. If you are an omnivore at no time does your mind stop to wonder where the meat is. Those who require a side of ranch to dip their pizza in will be in heaven as this herbaceous, flavor-forward sauce will have you wanting this over the dairy-packed version any day of the week.

Those in the know follow the cart on social media for the latest special and sold out notices. Baby

Baby Blue Pizza is often referred to when discussing Portland's best pizza, vegan or not.

Blue set out to create vegan pizza that leaves a lasting impression; after having any of their offerings, you'll be telling them job well done.

5 TOV COFFEE & TEA

Where else but Portland can you sip strong Egyptian coffee in a repurposed double-decker bus? Either cozy or cramped, depending on whether you see the glass as half empty or half full, **TOV COFFEE & TEA** offers as many coffee options as any brick and mortar coffee shop in a one-of-a-kind setting. In addition to the Egyptian-style coffees, which are brewed with cardamom, adding notes of citrus, mint, and spice, there are

distinct signature drinks that show that it is not just the quirky setting that draws people in.

On a hot day, try the signature Mint Thing, a combination of cold brew, mint, and cream. By popular request, they even started canning it! The Mucho Caliente sets itself apart with powerful spice notes of Peruvian *aji pancha* chile mixed with dark chocolate.

Order on the first floor, which has been converted to the bar where a purple, powder coat painted espresso machine matches the colored walls. Watch as your barista creates your drink with the focus of a master craftsman.

You could hang out in some of the few seats available on the first floor, but let's face it: Everyone comes to lounge on the rooftop patio. Decor will change depending on the season. Heavier awnings and heat lamps are out in the colder months, making it still enjoyable to dine at a cart in the winter in Portland, a rare feat to accomplish.

6

CUBO

Serving homestyle Cuban comfort food in an open casual setting is the name of the game for the food cart turned brick and mortar El Cubo de Cuba, or **CUBO** for short. They emphasize giving vegans and those who are gluten free plenty of options. It goes beyond merely offering their delicious bowls and salads as gluten-free options; they even offer gluten-free bread for celiacs, allowing them to

get in on the much talked-about Cubano sandwich.

Their drink menu has a strong focus on rum-based classics like mojitos and daiquiris, which go well with everything. The expansive patio gives plenty of room to enjoy your Havana Sunrise with a plate of *ropa vieja*, one of the national dishes of Cuba consisting of shredded beef and veggies.

Bright yellow walls with years of customers' signatures give sense of the community created. What's not to like? Relaxed, inviting atmosphere with food so good you can save some of the money you'd spend on your ticket to Cuba and spend it on another round at Cubo.

Save even more by hitting up one of their multiple happy hours that run Monday through Thursday from 3 to 6 p.m. and 9 to 10 p.m. as well. Rum cocktails go for only $5, and those who just want a lighter portion can nab any of their half sandwiches for $5 as well. Revolutions may have been had in Cuba, but if you come to Cubo you can taste a food revolution in each bite.

7 OK OMENS

A wine-focused bar with top-notch food, **OK OMENS** brings more good news than their name suggests. Despite the impressive resume chef Justin Woodward has from working at some of the most exclusive, innovative, fine-dining restaurants in New York, here he makes all welcome by taking the same level of care and execution and applying it to approachable favorites like chicken Caesar salad but at an elevated level. Want to try the fanciest combo meal ever? Order their burger, fries, and the aptly named "kinda like a McFlurry." While they can make more than a delicious chicken, the Szechuan peppercorns that stud the outside of each piece of poultry keep the lip-smacking tingle on your taste buds lingering longer and make it one time where it is adventurous to order the chicken.

Trickling over from their fine-dining sister restaurant, Castagna, the excellent standards go beyond the food; they have a drink selection so

good, *Food & Wine* magazine recently added them to their 100 Best Wine Restaurants list. Little quips throughout the menu inject some humor. The happy hour drink section titled "Some of the best cheap wines by the glass ever" consistently surprises and delights guests with wines that taste too good to be affordable, yet usually are less than $7 a glass. Can't decide between red or white? Go for a few wine bumps, a mini tasting flight of red, rosé, and white for $3 a shot. Nothing is over $25 on the dinner menu, and with their happy hour menus running twice a day, every day, and all day Sunday, there are so many opportunities to catch a great deal on items that are already a great deal to begin with. All signs point to OK Omens.

TIP

Buy natural wine for $36 per bottle, because real wine doesn't have to be expensive.

8

BARK CITY BBQ

In the food-service business it is all about location, location, location! And since one of Portland's most well regarded barbecue joints moved a little closer to where the action is, lines have not stopped forming for pitmaster and owner Michael Keskin's delicious smoked meats. Located in the Asylum food cart pod on Hawthorne, **BARK CITY BBQ** offers an array of goodies all smoked on Oregon Oak, giving the meat a distinct flavor not found in other regional barbecue.

Typically sides at barbecue joints never hold up to the main star; however this is not the case at Bark City. With unique sides like pickled avocado that cut through the fattiness of the smoked meat with a balance of bright acidity, you know you are in for something special. Chef Michael's sides are done so well they are often raved about as much as the proteins.

His St Louis ribs, sausages, and pulled pork have gained the attention of *Food & Wine* magazine. After years of experience at some of Portland's most revered barbecue restaurants, he creates a personal style that picks the best aspects of regional specialties to create a unique barbecue plate that one can describe as the best of everything. In a city where a barbecue scene is starting to emerge, Bark City continues to raise the bar for anyone trying to break in and take a piece of the pie. Despite all these accolades and attention, most days you can still find Chef Michael running the wheel, smiling at guests, knowing what flavor fireworks are heading their way.

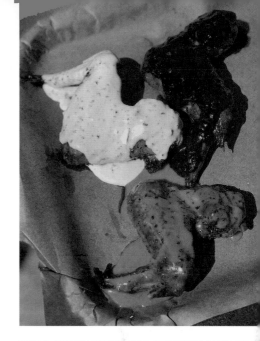

TIP

If you see the banana pudding milkshake on the menu, save room for it!

THE DIVISION CRAWL

1. **SCOTTIE'S PIZZA PARLOR,** 2128 SE Division St., (971) 544-7878, scottiespizzaparlor.com

2. **REEL M INN,** 2430 SE Division St., (503) 231-3880

3. **STELLA TACO,** 3060 SE Division St., (503) 206-5446, stellatacopdx .com

4. **PDX SLIDERS,** 3010 SE Division St., (503) 719-5464, pdxsliders.com

5. **LITTLE BEAST BREWING,** 3412 SE Division St., (503) 208-2723, littlebeastbrewing.com

6. **OUI! WINE BAR + RESTAURANT,** 2425 SE 35th Pl., (503) 208-2061, sewinecollective.com

7. **PINOLO GELATO,** 3707 SE Division St., (503) 719-8686, pinologelato .com

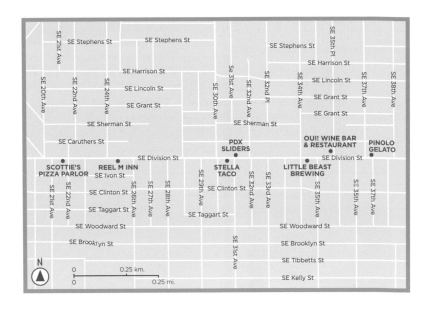

Old school meets new school

SOUTHEAST DIVISION HAS BECOME A MICROCOSMIC EXAMPLE of the change occurring throughout Portland. While some classic mainstays keep the ball rolling, newly constructed high rise apartments leave retail and restaurant space on the ground floor that provides some of the best spots in Southeast Portland to imbibe and unwind. Drink at a beer garden that used to be someone's residential garden before strolling down the road for fried chicken that we promise is worth the wait. You can ball out on a surprisingly affordable tasting menu that supersedes its value, or keep it low key with some comfort classics like tacos, pizza, burgers, and some of the best gelato the Pacific Northwest has to offer.

1

SCOTTIE'S PIZZA PARLOR

SCOTTIE'S PIZZA PARLOR is the culmination of a lifetime love affair between Scottie and pizza. Originally an East Coast kid, when his mother moved him away from Brooklyn to New Mexico as a child it became distinctly clear that not everywhere in the world has great pizza on every corner. The scarcity of good pizza in Albuquerque sent him on a path to learn to make the best pizza possible. Through a combination of self-education via the internet, time spent in pizza shops throughout the country, bouncing from New Mexico to New Haven, and finally landing in Oregon, Scottie found his calling, opening this casual, inviting counter-service spot with a cause.

While anyone can come in and order a slice, literally anyone, even those without the financial means, can dine at Scottie's thanks to their "Pay It

Forward" program, which allows customers to prepay for slices that then allow the less fortunate to dine with dignity. Aside from all the good feels you will get by paying it forward, their pizza alone will have you feeling over the moon.

Fresh, high-quality ingredients are on every pizza. One of their signature pies is the DeFino (named after his grandma), a square pie with fresh mozzarella, basil, oregano, garlic oil, pecorino romano, and tomato sauce, is highly sought after, partially because this is a highly labor-intensive pizza. They can only make 15 per day so get it while you can! Everything from their pepperoni to their seasonal pizzas can be purchased all the time. Even if there is a line, this efficient team makes it all happen in a timely manner with smiles on their faces. Good pizza, made with love that stands for some good causes. Scottie's Pizza Parlor does not just stand out for its pizza, but how they make a conscious effort to positively impact their community.

2 REEL M INN

What sounds like a bait shop with a corny name actually is a friendly dive bar with some of the best fried chicken in town. People plan their day around the most optimal time to hit up **REEL M INN**, because the waits for these birds can stretch long enough for you to not feel bad about ordering an extra drink or two (or three). Don't skip the *jojos*, the most perfectly cooked potato wedges to complement fried chicken ever. To kill time hit up the usually free pool table, but be cautious of your drinking neighbors nearby as it can be a tight squeeze. Once that time has passed your super crispy, juicy fried chicken will make its way to you with an array of dipping sauces to make those potatoes and birds sing.

Besides killer fried chicken, and yes it is organic, this tiny dive bar sets itself apart from newer spots by offering something that never goes out of style: great service. It's a small spot that often has just one person doing it all; sometimes it is even the owner herself! Regardless of who the person behind the bar is, they will make you feel like a regular even if it's your first time, all while hustling to get your drinks and make sure you are taken care of. In a town where sometimes you can feel like you are getting the cold shoulder, it is a warm welcome and a bit unexpected with its old-school, slightly punk vibe.

Restaurant folks frequently flock here, so act cool if you happen to see someone you followed on *Top Chef*. If you feel like something other than Rainier tallboys, the tap list will have something local and delicious for you so beer snobs and easygoing folks can drink in peace together. Whether you grew up around the corner, or are staying in town for a quick trip, all are welcome at the Reel M Inn.

TIP

Call ahead to see how long the current chicken wait is.

3

STELLA TACO

Wait, did we trip and fall into the Lone Star State? **STELLA TACO**, one of Portland's premier Tex-Mex taco shops, gets the little things right as owners Becky and Ian Atkins hail from that place where the stars at night are big and bright. Ahead of the curve on the current trend of Portland, they have been offering Austin-style breakfast tacos since 2016. While all their soft, street-style tacos can be made on corn tortillas should you want, we recommend you make at least one of yours "Texas style," which swaps out the corn tortilla for a house-made flour one and is topped with queso.

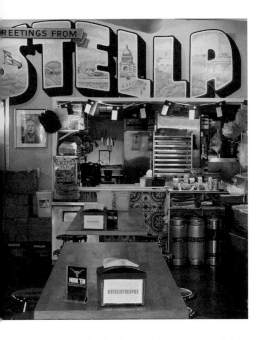

Affordable drinks are available all the time; however their happy hour is available Monday through Friday 3 to 6 p.m., when drink discounts make that frozen margarita taste even better. If you can't make it for happy hour, there are also daily specials offered. They mix things up from time to time with specials on certain days; all can be found posted on their social media accounts. Previous examples include fried chicken tacos, crispy shelled tacos, and even a Frito pie special. In addition to all that, if it happens to be your birthday, get ready to celebrate with an order of nachos on the house!

4

PDX SLIDERS

From a single food cart to brick and mortars throughout the city, **PDX SLIDERS** is killing the mini burger game. Slide in for a perfect quick bite as you head on down Division. Go nuts ordering a bunch of different sliders or stick to a single, but it is hard to choose just one. Each option is aptly named after a different bridge in Portland, and these sliders are not limited to just beef. The Marquam (smoked corn beef) or the Tillikum (buttermilk fried chicken) make for great non-traditional sliders. Go eclectic with the beefy Hawthorne, which includes bacon, goat cheese, and strawberry preserves, or try the braised pork on the Broadway.

If you just want a full-sized version, aka a regular burger, they can make that happen for you in any style offered. Go big with double beef on the Steel, smothered in cheese that will be running down your hands.

Weekly specials keep the kitchen on their toes and run long enough for you not to feel rushed to get it. Simple salads and fresh hand-cut fries round out the menu. If so inclined, you can turn your regular fries, with truffle salt and fresh parsley, into loaded fries from a couple options.

With a full bar there are plenty of options for an adult beverage to complement any food choice. If you happen to be at an event where you spot their catering truck, know that their consistency does not lack when they are away from home. Top-tier burger, low-tier price point.

5

LITTLE BEAST BREWING

What once was someone's home is now home to **LITTLE BEAST BREWING**, one of the area's newest breweries that specializes in really interesting beers brewed from cultures found in flora natural to the Pacific Northwest. Those cultures are what life and business partners Charles Porter and Brenda Crow refer to as the "little beasts" that duke it out to create the unique flavor profiles of their lineup. While an easy drinking Czech-style pilsner can be found on tap to enjoy anytime, make sure to save some room for one of their more distinct suds. The Pomme Sour takes the unique notes of apple, citrus, and vanilla found in quince and infuses it into a delicious farmhouse-style beer. Have a naturally sour red ale or a high-altitude Saison. Overwhelmed by all the interesting options? Get a flight and find out which is your new favorite.

A concise food menu offers salads and sandwiches, as well as a few smaller bites to snack on. Different areas give you the option of multiple

indoor and outdoor spots to post up and enjoy your adult bevvies; the main interior is split by a long, hardwood bar that runs the length of the house, but the expansive, multilevel patio gives more opportunities for groups to grab a table, or even surround the fire pit out front. We have even seen people bring their own blanket and set up shop on the front lawn to enjoy their beers.

6 OUI! WINE BAR + RESTAURANT

OUI! WINE BAR + RESTAURANT, found inside SE Wine Collective, a 5,000-square-foot urban winery, is one of those spots with no weak points. A lot of places have either a wine list so good, or food so great that you can forgive their transgressions elsewhere. Oui! slaps them all in the face by making the elusive attainable. The staff's relaxed confidence with no air of pretension lets you know you're in good hands.

If you want to ball out but are on a budget, forget the naysayers and say yes to Oui! Killer wines and one of the best deals on a chef's tasting menu in town should be enough to have you put this book down and book it over, but since you are still reading, let's continue.

Oui! is open for dinner, including several happy hours as well as family-style prix fixe menus and shareable plates all whipped up by the crazy talented chef Althea Grey Potter and crew. If you show up on the weekends, there is more time that happy hour is happening than not. Friday and Saturday nights there is a second happy hour from 10 to 11 p.m., the only time to get the half-baked sea salt chocolate chip cookie topped with sweet cream ice cream and house-made caramel.

Not sure which bottle to pop? No sweat: There are over 60 bottles offered by the glass so you can find something that calls to you without having to commit to a whole bottle. The collective's winemakers, Kate and Tom, can often be found on the floor chatting with guests, providing a rare opportunity to speak directly with the winemaker. At first glance, the menu may seem like items that you could get at a lot of wine bars, but this is the best version of that dish ever. They buck the notion that super Instagrammable plates lack flavor with offerings that pack a mean punch without sacrificing any beauty.

Althea holds a magical power of taking fresh-from-the-garden produce and making the plates somehow taste like crave-worthy junk food. If Mom could have made broccoli taste this good during our childhoods, we all would be eating way more of it. The menu constantly changes throughout the year to get the freshest offerings at the height of the season. What does not change is Althea's consistent bold flavors.

PINOLO GELATO

PINOLO GELATO offers real gelato from real Italians with the goal of using the best local ingredients to make the best product. But isn't gelato just Italian ice cream? Kind of, but not really. Without getting too technical, gelato has less fat and is not as cold as ice cream, which gives it a creamier texture, and the flavor is a more in-your-face punch because your tongue isn't freezing over as you eat it.

Co-owner Sandro Paolini re-creates the memories of eating gelato growing up in Tuscany with high-quality ingredients grown nearby. This philosophy is something co-owner Ashe Lyon can get behind after growing up living the farm life in eastern Oregon. With the abundance of rich soil, amazing product seems to pop up everywhere in the Pacific Northwest. Sometimes the basil even comes from his backyard! If it sounds like this is a recurring theme in Portland, there's a reason: There is so much good stuff here!

There is always a mix of made fresh daily seasonal flavors and mainstays on the board, but whatever you choose you cannot go wrong. The depth of flavor in their hazelnut gelato is super fresh, and since Oregon produces most of the hazelnuts in the United States, you best believe they got first dibs on the prime hazelnut action. Those that live that dairy-free life will not feel left out as there are an array of seasonal sorbettos. Needing that pick me up while getting your sugar fix? Order an affogato using Cafe Umbria's espresso. A scoop of Italian life on Division, that's amore.

TIP

You may catch their super cute pushcart around town and popping up at events.

THE DOWNTOWN CRAWL

1. **SHIFT DRINKS,** 1200 SW Morrison St., (503) 922-3933, shiftdrinkspdx
   .com

2. **LARDO,** 1205 SW Washington St., (503) 241-2490, lardosandwiches
   .com

3. **SANTERIA,** 703 SW Ankeny St., (503) 956-7624, santeriapdx
   .business.site

4. **MAMA CHOW'S KITCHEN,** 313 SW 2nd Ave.

5. **LECHON,** 113 SW Naito Pkwy., (503) 219-9000, lechonpdx.com

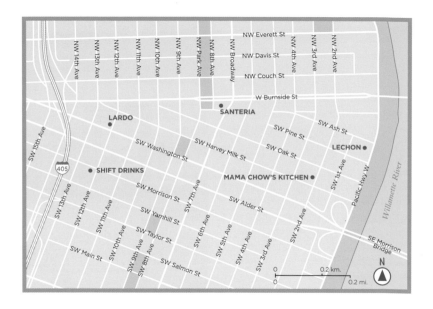

Downtown

Beep boop boppin' around, from the early morn 'til the break of dawn

WHEN IT'S TIME TO HANDLE BUSINESS, it's time to get downtown. But what about fun? Weekends turn Chinatown into club central where diners flood a bevy of spots to grab a quick bite before seeing a show, or just going hard on tasting menus from nationally acclaimed chefs. While the west side is more commercial than residential, it is not just bumbling tourists bumping into each other—but do watch out for them as they tend to not pay attention to traffic lights, probably because they are so enamored with the city, as Portland is often referred to as a playground for adults. Downtown offers recently renovated hotels offering go-to spots housing some of the best chefs in the city, as well as a plethora of food carts. A large number of carts have been displaced as the city grows, so as much as we are fans of food carts, it was hard to include many as there is much uncertainty when it comes to downtown carts and their long-term locations.

1

SHIFT DRINKS
No matter what time you get off the clock, it is time for a shift drink. The brainchild of a trio of Portland service industry vets, this bar is owned and operated by Alise Moffatt, Anne Garcia, and Anthony Garcia. **SHIFT DRINKS** came to be to combat the lack of after-work hangouts for industry patrons downtown. Shift Drinks has created an all day, every day happy hour; because in a town where most do not seem to abide

by the nine to five work life, and happy hour is meant to be a great deal for those just finishing their work day, why limit it to an hour? Instead let everyone get a deal, no matter what time they clock out. Any time of day there is a selection of snacks and adult drinks to make your wallet and your taste buds equally satisfied. While the Cubano sandwich may seem overdone as a bar menu item these days, the team at Shift Drinks makes an excellent rendition with perfectly crisped bread housing all the classic accoutrements: pickles, pork, mustard, and cheese. Whatever your cocktail heart desires can be made from the expansive bar, but let the pros do their thing and order something off the signature cocktail menu.

Aside from all the great deals, expansive wine list, and incredibly spacious seating area, Shift Drinks really is about the community and keeping it local. The relationships these pros developed can only be created through a lifetime of being in the biz; guests reap the benefits of the best local purveyors because they want to support people they believe in. Everything they offer is something they believe in from people they believe in; basically they have been in Portland since before it became the hyperlocal Portland it is today, and they have been able to cultivate relationships

with everyone who's anyone before they were somebody. Try a bite, enjoy a drink; you may even be rubbing elbows with the person that distilled your gin at Shift Drinks.

2 LARDO

LARDO is the "Cinderella story" that is told to all Portland food cart owners. Once upon a time, in a food cart pod on Belmont, a chef named Rick Gencarelli decided to create a little cart dedicated to delicious, pork-centric sandwiches and french fries served dirty that would make you happy to clean your plate. That little cart has grown up into the local juggernaut it is today with multiple locations throughout the city and even Las Vegas. When you are riding around downtown, be sure to take a sando break to get all the material you'd ever need for sandwich porn for your next Instagram post.

The tight menu changes throughout the year, so if you make it and don't see your favorite, it will find its way home. Certain sandwiches are year-round mainstays, like the "Egg Rick Muffin," Gencarelli's homage to the breakfast sandwich so many love in the a.m., served all day and with way better quality ingredients. American cheese is melted on top of an over medium egg and sausage patty housed on an English muffin made by

local bakery Dos Hermanos, and it even comes with a hash brown on the side! There are always vegetarian burger and chicken options for those who want something other than pork, but whatever you choose, do not skip on the fries. House-made and topped with Parmesan cheese and fried herbs, they make for an elevated side. If you are feeling extra, make them an order of dirty fries and let the crew top those bad boys with pickled peppers and big ol' chunks of pork belly.

Feeling guilty about all those calories you are stuffing down? Do good by eating good and order the monthly Chefwich, where each month a local chef creates a sandwich offered at all locations for a month and a dollar from each one is donated to a nonprofit of that chef's choosing. MF Tasty even got to get in on the action raising over $2,600 for Dollar For, a Pacific Northwest–based nonprofit that helps those overwhelmed by medical debt. Fun bites made by people who you can tell are having fun doing so is the vibe at Lardo.

Rick Gencarelli is also owner of neighboring pasta restaurant Grassa, as well as Beer O'Clock, which allows food from both establishments in it. Be on the lookout for the Kingpin pop-up, which solely focuses on East Coast–style lobster rolls and often has devout lines of people waiting for one.

3 SANTERIA

Some magic is brewing downtown, and it is happening at **SANTERIA**. This unique little Mexican restaurant has little twists on an all too common story. So many chefs credit cooking with Grandma as how they learned their craft; however at Santeria, the owner's "abuela" that taught him all his knowledge happened to be a drag queen instead of a little old lady. With a shoestring budget of just $4,000, this spot took over a sliver of space next to one of Portland's oldest strip clubs named Mary's, and from four in the afternoon until late into the evening people can come for pints of margaritas, giant burritos, and standout fish tacos. Dine in or take it next door to Mary's for dinner and a show. While minors are not allowed in the club, the only funny business your kid may see in the dining room is a wet

burrito the size of their torso land in front of them. Some owners work themselves out of a job, but here you can find the owner, Wade, working the line most nights. Even if meat is not your thing, there are plenty of vegetarian and vegan options. Portions are on the bigger side, giving the perfect opportunity to share with a friend or tap out and have your lunch for the next day already handled. Industry folks get an extra 10 percent off their bill, and everyone gets hooked up with free chips and salsa if you order a drink. Quirky yet cozy, the name may say Santeria on the door, but the magic is in the flavorful food.

TIP

Get Wade's favorite burrito: chicken tinga upgraded with guacamole and sour cream.

4 MAMA CHOW'S KITCHEN

Whether it is your lunch break from work, or you are just down for some good eats, **MAMA CHOW'S KITCHEN** on 2nd Avenue downtown is worth hopping over to. Bay Area restaurant vet Jeff Chow channels the comfort food of Mom into a tight menu of bangers for the person on the go. Roll up to this food cart that looks more like a tiny house for a little comfort from Mama Chow. A concise menu offers lollipop chicken wings, as well as Kahlúa pork that can be served over steamed rice or garlic noodles, as well as Mama's signature dumplings. Do not sleep on the garlic noodles! They are addictively flavorful, and let's be honest, noodles are always more exciting than steamed rice. The other standout is the chicken-stuffed dumplings that can be found a few ways. As the weather cools down, diners

TIP

Do not stroll in at the last hour expecting the whole menu, as they tend to sell out daily. While they have not made it into all the food blogs, they do have a cult following for their dumplings. First-time customers will innocently ask why don't they just buy more, not realizing they are all handmade.

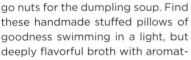

go nuts for the dumpling soup. Find these handmade stuffed pillows of goodness swimming in a light, but deeply flavorful broth with aromatics and herbs. Whichever combo you choose, not only will your taste buds be happy, but your wallet as well.

The very limited seating is not so much of an issue as scenic places like Tom McCall Waterfront are a hop, skip, and a jump away, giving you expansive views of the Willamette and East Portland while you get down on your grub. Go ahead and get that noodle pull picture with beautiful Portland in the background. The big-ticket item is their combo of pretty much everything, which gets you all the most popular items; this is the way to go. Hours are limited to daytime, Monday through Friday, so make sure to carve some time out of your week to pay a visit to Mama Chow.

5

LECHON

Standing alone is not the only thing that makes **LECHON** stand out. You are not likely to stroll past their location, but it is worth putting this address in your GPS and finding this wood-fired South American spot. This well-designed eatery boasts so many areas for you to sit and relax: either inside by the ginormous fish tank, or outside on their patio where views of the Willamette River are across the street. See all the activity at Tom McCall Waterfront Park as you sip on your Mal Humorado, a tequila

cocktail that features passion fruit and habañero syrup and is an even better deal during the happy hour offered daily.

The menu offers ceviches, wood-fired eats, and seafood. A simple dish like bread and chimichurri may sound basic, but their version is quite the opposite. Maybe it is the extra depth of flavor from the wood-fired grill, maybe it's the high-class vibe, but something makes it superior. The happy hour shrimp ceviche is plated like a dish at a Michelin star restaurant and tastes just as fancy; pops of bright heat from *aji amarillo* play off the sweetness of the seafood leaving you wanting to slurp up every bite. Big spenders can enjoy a 28-day dry-aged ribeye, or eat like a king off the expansive happy hour menu.

This is not just another South American restaurant; it's a place to experience great renditions of classic and new dishes that make you feel like you took a trip across the hemisphere while actually taking in the sights of lovely Portland.

THE BONUS COFFEE CRAWL

1. **IN J COFFEE**, 1431 SW Park Ave., (971) 270-6856, injcoffee.com

2. **CAFFE UMBRIA**, 710 SW Madison, (503) 719-5248, caffeumbria.com

3. **DEADSTOCK COFFEE**, 408 NW Couch St., (971) 220-8727, deadstockcoffee.com

4. **LA PERLITA**, NW 9th Ave.721 NW 9th Ave.

5. **NOSSA FAMILIA COFFEE**, 1350 NW Lovejoy St., (541) 304-9234, nossacoffee.com

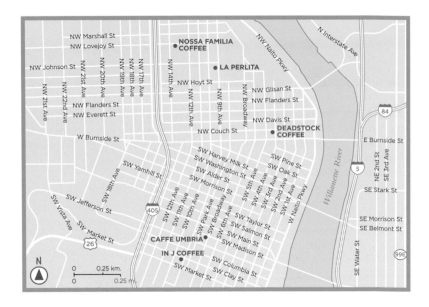

Bonus Crawl!

Coffee: It's kind of a big deal

PORTLAND DOESN'T SLEEP WHEN IT COMES TO THEIR COFFEE game. Practically any spot in town is brewing something amazing from a local roaster. So to stand out, you must bring something truly exceptional. All shops here offer something a cut above the rest in a city with already high coffee standards. To keep you going while bouncing around downtown, each of these spots offers their own unique take on the beans that keep the world working.

1 IN J COFFEE

Playful from the get-go, **IN J COFFEE** wants you to enjoy some coffee from them! See what they did there? Paying homage to owner Joe Yang's Chinese heritage, they roast their own special blend featuring Chinese Yunnan beans, making them the only shop to feature this region of the world's coffee. After moving to Portland from China three years ago, Joe got a job as a barista learning the coffee business while simultaneously learning

English. Already a skilled barista, with awards under his belt for his exceptional latte art and coffee-brewing expertise, Joe used these skills to segue into the American market. When he felt confident in his new city, he opened In J, which is the first Chinese-owned coffee shop in Portland.

Aside from a standout origin story, the specialty drinks created here stand out as well. Try the Zao latte which features date jam as well as a textured garnish of dried dates that looks almost like bits of granola floating atop the latte art,

but gives way to a sweet, chewy texture that truly sets this coffee apart from the typical coffee shop lineup. Little pastries from Rushmore Baking can accompany any drink you choose. An extra special treat is the Chinese Pig in a Blanket, made by a private baker, which takes the classic cocktail party snack to the next level with Chinese sausage wrapped in a sweeter dough. The spice from the sausage creates a perfect balance and is worth coming for on its own. While not always on the menu, if you see it on the board be sure to order it. It is easy to enjoy the exceptional, well-executed drinks and great service at In J.

2 CAFFE UMBRIA

Originating a little north in Seattle, **CAFFE UMBRIA** continues to bring its flair for Italian-style coffees to this region of the Pacific Northwest. Sourcing coffees globally to make the perfect blend, Umbria takes that variety in beans and funnels it through the Italian espresso bar experience. High ceilings with a blend of natural and focused lighting make the hues of color pop in the cleanly decorated cafe. Sleek details line the space with gold accents and checkerboard tiled floors. The coffee standards are all here and done very well. Should you love the java but want to run on your own time, we suggest stocking up on the cans of their own cold-brew coffee to have later or while on the go. Special blends can be found during community events throughout the city like Portland's Negroni week, where you can find the balance of bitterness and sweet found in the cocktail in the roast. This spacious and elegant space will have you feeling refined.

3

DEADSTOCK COFFEE

It ain't hard to tell, who excels then prevails. The tunes bump the best of hip-hop while the sneaker heads admire the partition made of Nike Air Jordans. In a town where the standard in coffee is already above most places, owner Ian Williams separates himself from the masses. **DEADSTOCK** offers "snob free" coffee, open to all with a refreshing cultural mantra of "Coffee Should Be Dope," and it is. Sneaker culture prevails with the house reading material packed with books showcasing the history of many

signature shoes and their progression throughout the years. You can even garnish your latte with shoe art of your choice: Jordans, Converse, Adidas, or Reebok. Williams spent time at Nike before breaking out to offer a coffee experience so popular that it has expanded to Tokyo. A strong sense of community is felt as regulars are greeted like long-lost family, where all congregate with a shared passion for sneaker culture and caffeine. Go for a cup, or take one of their signature roasts home with you. Thirsty but the coffee is not calling your name? Go for the refreshing LeBronald Palmer, a play on the classic Arnold Palmer featuring lemonade mixed with their coffee/sweet tea blend Zero Chill. While it has not been confirmed, it is rumored to be LeBron James's favorite drink and the version here is truly the taste of champions. If you happen to be in Chinatown and like coffee, sneakers, or both, this place is not to be missed.

4 LA PERLITA

What started as a side hustle has turned into a full-time gig for owner Angel Medina. While working his corporate job, he would sell small batches of his roasts for a $10 donation to United We Dream, the country's largest youth-led immigrant rights advocacy group. Demand got so big so quickly, they had to move production out of his apartment and into a proper space. Found in the lobby of the EcoTrust building, **LA PERLITA** offers rich cups of coffee from Small Time Roasters, their own roasting company. While their menu has all the classics, the specialty drinks are where your focus should be. The True Mexican Mocha is a flavor bomb that will gain you all the likes online from its stunning presentation that includes a rimmed mug studded with cocoa nibs and freeze-dried raspberries that burst on your tongue with each sip. The Cafe de Olla goes to other levels with its complexity using *piloncillo*, an unrefined Mexican sugar made from boiling and evaporating cane sugar juice. If you are not sure which one to pick, a Cortadito tasting flight will get you a Cuban, a Brazilian, and a Mexican varietal of coffee for you to choose your favorite.

5

NOSSA FAMILIA COFFEE

NOSSA FAMILIA COFFEE, founded by Augusto Carneiro, links his passion for coffee roasting in Portland to his family's farms in Brazil. The origins of their sourcing began with directly buying from his family's farms, and now Nossa has expanded their offerings to other specialty coffees from Peru, Kenya, and beyond. As Oregon's first Certified B Corporation (a time-consuming certification that shows your company practices the utmost highest standards in sustainability), Nossa and all those in their supply chain practice sustainability in their sourcing, farming, and serving techniques, leaving you with a delicious cup of coffee that you can feel good about. All locations offer tastings every Saturday at

noon when you can educate yourself on different types of coffee and how they vary; learn what type of coffee you need in your life for free without committing to a million bags you may hate. The most photographed and talked about is their mocha, which in addition to the classic chocolate latte setup features a healthy topping of chocolate whip that will be sure to satisfy any chocophile. High ceilings in this two-story shop are lined with plants, breathing life into an industrial space. Hit up Nossa and help support the family biz.

THE BONUS DOWNTOWN HOTEL RESTAURANTS CRAWL

1. **KING TIDE**, 1510 SW Harbor Way, (503) 295-6166, kingtidefishandshell.com

2. **XPORT BAR & LOUNGE**, 1355 SW 2nd Ave., (503) 306-4835, xportportland.com

3. **URBAN FARMER**, 525 SW Morrison St., (503) 222-4900, urbanfarmerportland.com

4. **DEPARTURE**, 525 SW Morrison St., (503) 802-5370, departureportland.com

5. **ROSA ROSA**, 750 SW Alder St., (503) 294-9700, rosarosapdx.com

6. **BULLARD/ABIGAIL HALL**, 813 SW Alder St., (503) 222-1670, bullardpdx.com

7. **IL SOLITO**, 627 SW Washington St., (503) 228-1515, ilsolitoportland .com

8. **CRAFT PDX**, 320 SW Harvey Milk St., (971) 222-2111, hi-lo-hotel.com

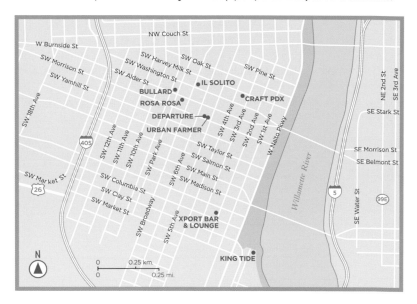

Bonus Crawl!

Downtown hotel restaurants

WITH THE EAST SIDE OF PORTLAND BEING HOME TO THE COOL, smaller independent restaurants, downtown Portland is hotel central. Typically to make everyone happy hotel restaurants subject travelers to the most mediocre versions of dishes that the masses would recognize. Perhaps because it is such a foodie town, this just will not fly in Portland. Downtown hosts the best hotels—most recently renovated—where the restaurants are so good the locals go, because let's face it, the people want the flavor fireworks. Big-name local chefs draw crowds for their bold flavors, each with their own distinct style. You can't beat stellar food, great service, and the ability to get a room and turn your night into a staycation.

KING TIDE

Is it a cliché to have a waterfront restaurant that focuses on seafood? Only if they phone it in with some run-of-the-mill versions of crowd favorites that have been done to death. Thank the food gods that **KING TIDE** has been saved from that fate and instead brings it full force with "Portland style" versions of American seafood classics. To us this style just means utilizing high-quality local products and not being afraid to have some fun while doing so. Thirsty? Make your choice from an array of options; the wines are local, the beer is cold, and the cocktails are all made with love.

Summertime is the right time to nab a seat on their patio, which gives views of the Willamette River as well as the Tom McCall Waterfront area. The

views are even more exceptional when accompanied by their unique take on a lobster roll, which breaks with tradition and instead houses all that lobster in a black brioche bun colored by squid ink. During the summer their Tacos + Tequila events are held at a cozy little satellite kitchen on their patio that has a few high-top seats for those who want an intimate view of all the action. Sourcing tortillas from Three Sisters, the premier local tortilla company, they serve freshly made tacos that tap into executive chef Lauro Romero's Mexican heritage as well as innovative ideas straight from the chef's mind. Even their chips and salsa game reaches new levels with these locally sourced tortillas offering a freshness usually overlooked by places that purchase mass-produced premade tortillas. Daily ceviches showcase the freshest things of the moment and are an even better steal during happy hour. Whatever the tide brings in, the team at King Tide will give it the royal treatment.

2

XPORT BAR & LOUNGE

Located on the rooftop at the Porter Hotel, this bar and lounge imports you upstairs and exports flavor bombs to your taste buds. The decor at **XPORT BAR & LOUNGE** may lead you to believe that you are entering a Vegas nightclub, but the relaxed vibe pairs well with the futuristic decor. In this version of the future, service is friendly and welcoming to all. Originally designed to be on the ritzy and exclusive side, the menu has become affordable and is welcomed by locals and travelers alike. The later the evening gets, the more upbeat the vibe and the younger the clientele. The vibe changes along with the lighting; one visit can feature a rainbow ceiling, while another can illuminate all pink or sky blue. See a bird's-eye view of the city from their covered patio. A mix of Asian-inspired and continental

classics are spread throughout the menu; you may find baba ghanoush alongside a pork katsu sandwich. Be sure to save room for dessert. The Shibuya Toast is a showstopper that features hazelnut milk jam, whipped mascarpone cheese, chocolate, and matcha ice cream. Beers and wines are on discount during happy hour, but if you want to go big, bottles of sparkling wine are discounted 20 percent! The big takeaway is you can feel like a baller without breaking the bank. Breathtaking views, and grown-ass vibes without grown-ass prices: Get out and go to Xport.

3

URBAN FARMER

While the term "farm to table" seems to be played out, the modern steakhouse inside the Nines hotel is far from some corporate spot playing off the popularity of buzzwords; they talk the talk and walk the walk. Direct sourcing from an array of local veggie slingers and ranchers give the guests at **URBAN FARMER** access to some of the freshest offerings from the Pacific Northwest prepared by executive chef Matt Christianson and his skilled staff. With a rooftop herb garden, beehives, and a mushroom-growing facility onsite, some of those fresh goodies never had to travel more than a few floors before landing on your plate. How's that for locally sourced?

The restaurant is decorated in a way that makes you feel like you are in a terrarium floating in the middle of the hotel. Steel frames hug the exterior of the dining room, with partitions separating sections stacked with jars filled with preserved veggies that will make it to your plate as rotation dictates, just like on the farm. Bright pops of color draw the eye to the expansive seating areas in the lounge, and give the diners many uniquely designed areas to get their fill of some house dry-aged meats.

Brunch time can be crunch time as they offer one of the most interesting Bloody Mary bars in the city, with a rotation of seasonally pickled garnishes made in-house that far exceed the basic, mass-produced stuff coming out of store-bought jars. Even with all these products sitting right at his fingertips, Chef Matt often visits the farmers' markets for those seasonal, small-batch finds that truly make him an urban farmer.

4

DEPARTURE

Get ready for takeoff. It's going to be a delicious flight. *Top Chef* fan favorite Gregory Gourdet's Southeast Asian flavors are enveloped by chic decor and breathtaking city views. Food runs the gamut of elevated (no pun intended for a rooftop location) street food to more filling entrees and market-fresh sushi. Grab a seat at the huge wrap-around bar set center stage in their main dining room, or head out to one of the two balcony patios to check out the panoramic views of PDX and see everyone in the middle of their hustle and bustle in the streets of downtown. Good for both the casual bite as well as those who want a chef-driven tasting menu, **DEPARTURE** has something for everyone.

Happy hour is the best time to drop in and get a taste without blowing your whole stack. Their sushi game is on point with signature hand rolls with a substantial amount of fish. Taking a bar classic and making it refined, their lollipop chicken wings give you that approachable snack in a way that will have you asking for seconds. Substantial noodles should be the name of a large-format pasta spot, but could aptly describe the filling portions served here. The happy hour Mahogany noodles sound simple but are deceptively rich in flavor, evoking memories of the best East Coast chow mein done through the eyes of someone with crazy culinary prowess. Drinks do not disappoint, with a large selection of wines by the glass, Japanese whiskeys and highballs, as well as signature drinks that keep with the

Pan Asian flair while paying respect to the ingredients. With happy hour, late-night, as well as regular dinner service, there seems to always be an opportunity to book a time to take a trip to Departure.

5

ROSA ROSA

Have you ever gone on a vacation that your mind just cannot forget? **ROSA ROSA** is the ongoing postcard to chef and restaurateur Vitaley and Kimberly Paley's summer travels through Europe. Located inside the Dossier hotel, Rosa Rosa takes us on a trip through the Ottoman Empire with dishes ranging from Turkish breads to a not so simple chicken that is an homage to the hotel restaurant they dined at while staying in the former Soviet republic of Georgia. The flavors chosen touch deeper than just a memorable family vacation as Vitaley and Kimberly both have family ties to that part of the world. Chicken Chkmeruli, a famous dish of pressed chicken from Hotel Zuzumbo in Telavi, Georgia, is showcased on the menu, but if you come during happy hour, you can try a smaller portion as a kebab. One

bite and you will understand why people travel to the hotel for the original, but save your plane fare and take a shorter commute to try this incredibly juicy, flavorful bird. The boyo is flaky bread layered with spinach and cheese, taking something so simple and maximizing the flavor from each ingredient. Hummus, which has been done to death on almost every menu, is brought to new life with green garbanzos; the less mature version of garbanzo beans picked before turning into the tan bean we all have known to love takes on an edamame-like flavor without the soy, leaving a unique flavor note to this silky whipped spread. Feel like you've skipped across the Atlantic while sipping on A Night in Tunisia, the signature happy hour drink which features gin, Campari, and spices, and happens to be on tap. The opulent Old World vibes go beyond the menu as the decor takes us to an era that has been long forgotten. No need for over the top furnishings when accented craftsmanship can be found in the intricately laid black and white checker tile floor and unique light fixtures. Old classics will become new favorites at Rosa Rosa.

6

BULLARD/ABIGAIL HALL

If it is tradition for all the *Top Chef* alumni to open standout restaurants in downtown hotels, chef Doug Adams's **BULLARD** carries on that tradition with pride. Making no apologies for its honest, flavor-forward Tex-Mex cuisine, Bullard welcomes you in and cooks with confidence. Expansive booths allow the largest of parties to feel like they have a space of their own. This is a great place for groups, not just because of the large seating but because the menu is formatted in a way that makes larger plates

easy to share. Or you can grab a bunch of smaller plates and have a plethora of bites to compare and contrast. Elevated versions of items familiar to most can be found, such as tostadas that use premium seafood like day boat albacore tuna or grilled scallops. Deceptively simple tamales give over-the-top flavors from a deep, rich Texas red chili poured on top. The smoker is working overtime to give some great larger dishes like pork belly for two, 16-ounce ribeyes, and flavorful apps like dry-rubbed chicken wings. Wet your whistle with exceptionally done classics, pickle-back pairings, and even their own lager. Should you want a little more intimate area for a drink and a nibble, go around the corner to **ABIGAIL HALL**, the sister

cocktail lounge that keeps the kitchen in the family to give you a second area to enjoy those standout bites. Sip, sip hooray with even more cocktails to choose from and one hell of a burger that is even more celebratory when it's happy hour; because everything tastes better at a discount. Don't sleep on brunch because of these three words: fried chicken tacos!

IL SOLITO

Located inside the trendy, yet sophisticated Kimpton Hotel Vintage Portland, Il Solito—led by chef Matt Sigler and his team—puts out some of the best Italian food in town. Each Kimpton hotel location creates a restaurant concept around their executive chef, as opposed to the opposite, and the identity of **IL SOLITO** heavily follows Sigler's career. He previously worked

for some of the top places in San Francisco like Quince and Flour + Water before traveling through Colombia and Italy, where he focused on pastas, whole animal butchery, and charcuterie making. These aspects shine in Il Solito's menu. While the effort to make these dishes is no joke, the chefs make it seem like it is all fun and games in the kitchen. Il Solito translates to "the usual," meaning Sigler wants to take you down memory lane but with elevated technique. Lighthearted familiar dishes and East Coast Italian-American classics are sprinkled throughout the menu. Tender meatballs roll around to a few options, but if you happen to catch happy hour in the bar, get the burger which features a mouth-watering meatball patty that leaves nothing to be desired but a second order! House-made mozzarella

TIP

Belly up to Bacchus Bar in the lobby, where you can complement your cocktails with a small menu of offerings from Il Solito.

sticks are an artisanal play on everyone's favorite chain appetizer; on the outside it looks like the run-of-the-mill frozen classic, but inside bursts with house-made mozzarella and a depth of seasoning reserved for things far classier than fried cheese.

As it is a hotel restaurant, breakfast, lunch and dinner is offered every day. Be sure to get at least one pasta dish for your table, and if you've

already experienced that happy hour meatball goodness, go for the corn ravioli if it happens to be on the menu. The extensive wine and beer selection makes it hard to choose just one drink. Should you want a cocktail, superb versions of classics as well as original concoctions made by Nathan Elliot and team will make you forget all your problems on your first sip. Il Solito has cultivated great relationships with local farmers to bring the best of each season. Whether you're just having the usual or trying something new, Il Solito offers those who venture downtown a taste of the finer life that all can enjoy.

8

CRAFT PDX

However you view cooking, you have to respect the **CRAFT PDX**. Chef Bryant Kryck and team pair classic American dishes with the best quality local ingredients the Pacific Northwest has to offer to give guests something familiar, but at a standard above what they are used to. Typically hotel restaurants err on the corporate side, leaving little room for creativity for the chef running the show; this is not the case as the Hi Lo Hotel steps back and lets Chef Bryant put his signature on the menu. No need for a lab coat when entering the Burger Lab, which allows guests to customize America's

fan favorite to their liking. Think Smashburger meets fine dining with this custom blend of brisket, chuck, and short ribs made to order and placed on a local Grand Central Bakery potato bun. Those with an aversion to gluten can sub out a gluten-free bun. Before choosing from a library of toppings, decide on one, two, or even three patties that all include your choice of cheese, as well as peppercorn aioli and arugula, but who wants to stop at that? While

there are additional toppings that include a variety of extra cheese, sauces, and pickled things, the premium toppings are what sets this apart from any run-of-the-mill "build your own burger" setup. Crispy bay shrimp, local veggies, and mac-and-cheese stand out in addition to plenty of meat-centric add-ons like bacon, brisket, or even smoked chicken. Craft PDX uses local meat mavens Nicky USA, and the custom meat blends set a higher standard for all their meat offerings.

Happy hour not only offers deals on regular menu items, but rotating specials make their way on and off the discounted menu. Bay shrimp with aioli, cocktail sauce, and bread not only makes a carb-friendly version of shrimp cocktail, but also is a childhood dish Chef Bryant grew up on. Make a meal out of a handful of happy hour options or splurge on one of their seasonal specials; either way your taste buds will be happy. While based in the lobby of a hotel, you will find yourself feeling like you are in a stand-alone restaurant that is just as inviting for locals to pop in and enjoy.

THE PEARL CRAWL

1. **NOLA DOUGHNUTS**, 110 NW 10th Ave., (503) 895-6350, noladoughnuts.com

2. **POP BAGEL**, 433 NW 10th Ave., (971) 302-6110, popbagel.co

3. **ANDINA RESTAURANT**, 1314 NW Glisan St., (503) 228-9535, andinarestaurant.com

4. **KHAO SAN**, 1435 NW Flanders St., Ste. A, (503) 227-3700, khaosanpdx.com

5. **BOTANIST BAR PDX**, 1300 NW Lovejoy St., (971) 533-8064, botanistbarpdx.com

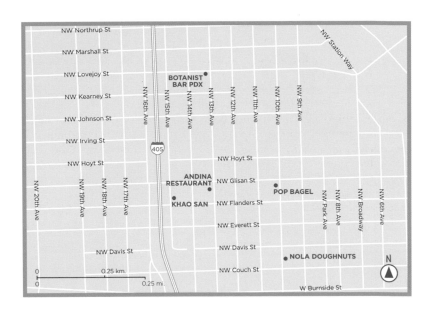

Pearl

Sleek eateries with quick, yet posh nosh

THEY SAY PORTLAND IS ALL FLANNEL SHIRTS and scraggly beards. While that style may be popular in the Pacific Northwest, the flannel in the Pearl district is most likely sourced from finer places. What once was a no man's land of warehouses has transformed into artist lofts, galleries, as well as larger-sized restaurants, bars, and breweries. Put on your finest Pendleton and hop from spot to spot. Have some of the richest bagels at the offshoot of a wildly popular patisserie that is steps away. Start your day with a coffee tasting, then bounce from a temple of Peruvian food to a subterranean bar serving innovative cocktails. Jackie Kennedy once said, "Pearls are always appropriate," and it is always an appropriate time to head over to the Pearl.

NOLA DOUGHNUTS

Sometimes it's hip to be square, and if you get one of the very special doughnuts from **NOLA**, it would be one of those times. What makes it so special? The team combined their Louisiana roots (LA) and croissant-like La'ssant dough, which requires a three-day process to make, to create some super flavorful, square-shaped doughnuts. Their Pelican State influence can be found throughout the menu with beignets, king cakes, and po'

TIP

Pair your doughnut with a hot chocolate, tea, or one of their locally sourced, small-batch coffee drinks.

boy sandwiches to make you feel like you're at Mardi Gras without the crowds. We can never order just one as all their flavors are so well executed our mouths keep watering while thinking about it. Get a fresh brûléed marshmallow on top of your S'mores, go with a classic glazed, or go nuts with Cajun Maple Bacon or Salted Double Chocolate Ganache. There is no wrong way to get your sugar fix while feeling a little fancy. The owners are doughnut enthusiast Frank, as well as brother and sister Rob and Connie, who still have fond memories growing up enjoying po' boy sandwiches at their family's second generation–owned restaurant run by their aunt and uncle in New Orleans. They pay attention to the small details in their po' boys to give every guest a taste of their childhood in each bite. We were skeptical about getting a tasty po' boy from a wildly tasty doughnut shop, but we took the risk so you don't have to. Rest assured you will be just as pleased with the po' boy as you will be with the doughnuts; they both even taste good the next day.

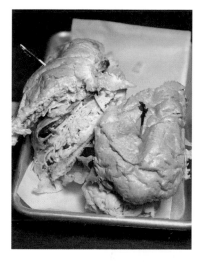

2 POP BAGEL

Steps away from Marius Pop's wildly popular patisserie Nuvrei, you can find some of the most uncommon and interesting bagels in the city. What makes these bagels linger on your mind days after eating is the pretzel dough base, not typically used in traditional bagels. Biting through the perfectly browned exterior gives way to a rich, chewy dough that has people drooling when remembering their trips to this shop. Depending on how simple or crazy you want to make it, **POP BAGEL** has you covered. There are at least a dozen types of bagels to choose from, be it plain, the perfect Everything, or something distinctive like Espresso Rye. Almost as many options are laid out for spreads. If you feel like you may get a case of FOMO ask and the staff will happily go half and half on your bagel; now you can try Kimchi Cream Cheese alongside some safe bets or out there flavors like Blueberry-Black Pepper. Be as fancy as you want to be, or turn one of those doughy masterpieces

into a bagel sandwich. Their cups of joe complement any food option. Simply put Pop Bagel is good for three things: bagels, sandwiches, and coffee; mission accomplished on all three.

3

ANDINA RESTAURANT

ANDINA is a family affair; some consider it to be the fourth child of owners John Platt and Doris Rodriguez de Platt, who met in the 1960s while John was traveling in Peru. After fate kept bringing them together, they married and moved back to Oregon to raise a family. Once their three sons had grown up, it was time for their fourth labor of love, the restaurant Andina, a tribute to Peru and a blend of North and South American cultures. These lovebirds are serious about getting those authentic flavors right. In the past they have paid to send their chefs to Peru to eat and work, learning the subtleties in flavor one can only get from dining there. While most would put a blanket description on this food and just call it Peruvian, Andina focuses specifically on *la cocina Criolla*, one of Peru's most popular styles of cuisine. It is an ever-evolving blend of newer techniques with classic dishes from the past. The quality is incredibly fresh as they not only work with a ton of local farmers and suppliers throughout Oregon, but also have set up direct trade routes with farmers in Peru for those ingredients you just can't find anywhere else.

The multistoried space has so much room for activities; if you're popping in for a quick bite or drink, head to the right and grab a seat at the expansive lounge and bar area. If you're feeling adventurous snack on their beef heart *anticuchos*. They have an assortment of these little skewers of meat for those who may be more conservative with their proteins. Their happy hour snacks include empanadas, but do not skip out on their *cebiche mango verde*, which features green mango and poached prawns tossed in a *leche*

de tigre that is so bright and refreshing you'll feel like you are in a sunny oasis regardless of season.

An extensive wine collection and cocktail menu complement the food; drinks focus on flavors of Latin America but expand beyond specifically Peru. While their bartenders can make you a fantastic margarita, we recommend the Pisco Sour or Sacsayhuaman cocktail; because when you're at a Peruvian spot owned by people from Peru, it just seems like the smart choice.

KHAO SAN

4

With dreams of bring-
ing the Thai street
food culture back
home to Portland,
owners Pounong and
Sumitar Saysouriyo-
sack—you can call them Nong and
Bud—decided to open a spacious,
airy spot named after the famous
street in Bangkok that is the premier spot for traveling backpack-
ers to get down on all the street
food goods. **KHAO SAN** is sprinkled
with items they brought back with
them from Thailand to keep an air

of authenticity. Examples include the furniture, the servers' uniforms, and the cooking equipment, but the pièce de résistance is the *tuk tuk* (Thai bicycle taxi) that has been converted into the booth that everyone wants to snag when they walk in. The menu is super affordable, with nothing over $20. Standouts include Ping, chargrilled skewers of either chicken or pork marinated in evaporated milk and served on a metal rack, a dish that is heavy on the presentation factor. Classics like papaya salad can be found with varying degrees of spiciness if requested. Wash it all down with an authentically Thai Chang beer, or if you want to skip the booze go for a Thai iced tea to keep your mouth happy and your body cool and refreshed.

5

BOTANIST BAR PDX

Of all the gin joints in all the towns in all the world, you should walk into this one. **BOTANIST BAR** is a subterranean bar with elements of terroir—plants, natural woods, and earthy green paint lets you know you are in for something special the second you walk down those stairs and open the front door. Urban Farmer protégé Robbie Wilson has made the type of place where classy, sexy drinks are available for all with an appreciation for quality: no formal wear required. While there is a focus on gin, the options do not stop there if that spirit isn't calling your name.

Experimental cocktail night on Tuesday features drinks so new that they are not even named yet! Help the badasses behind the bar choose their next signature beverage. Each drink has ingredients listed and is numbered. Maybe drink number three is the newest drink to sweep the nation, maybe it is just what works for that week, but there is always something new to keep you interested. If you are more of a traditionalist, their execution of the classics are on lock. Great, welcoming, and knowledgeable service helps those who are branching out from their go-to drink, or unsure of an ingredient. Even if it is your first time in, they will make you feel like you have been coming here for years. After one visit with friends we were recognized very quickly by master mixologist Ian when we returned for other visits. As is expected in Portland, food is not an afterthought. Everyone talks about the poke nachos: Fried and spiced wontons are topped with wakame, spicy mayo, avocado crema, sesame, and scallions. Come for the drinks, stay for a snack, meet some new friends; whatever you choose, you are in for something special at Botanist Bar.

THE ALPHABET DISTRICT CRAWL

1. **FISH & RICE**, 2332 NW Westover Rd., (503) 954-1270, fishnrice.com

2. **BHUNA**, 704 NW 21st Ave., (971) 865-2176, bhunarestaurant.com

3. **THE WAITING ROOM**, 2327 NW Kearney St., (503) 477-4380, thewaitingroompdx.com

4. **MOBERI**, 1755 NW 23rd Ave., (503) 890-9333, moberi.com

5. **LIFE OF PIE**, 1765 NW 23rd Ave., (503) 820-0083, lifeofpiepizza.com

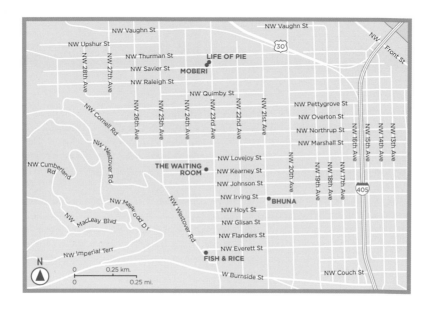

Alphabet District

From OG chefs and mainstays
to some new players on the block

THE JACKSON 5 SANG "ABC, EASY AS 1, 2, 3," and the Alphabet District of Portland is almost that easy to navigate. Stroll down the streets and you will notice that each one starts with a letter of the alphabet and progresses in order. Head past Everett Street to Flanders, and so on. Should you lose your way, the letters going higher in the alphabet head north; make your way back to Burnside (the street that divides North from South Portland), and you will notice the streets descending in alphabetical order. Some spots have been around for years, while others have made their debut more recently and already are the talk of the town. Now that you've learned your ABCs, stroll the streets and grab a taste from these.

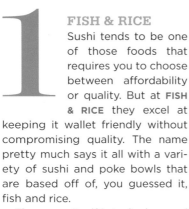

1

FISH & RICE

Sushi tends to be one of those foods that requires you to choose between affordability or quality. But at **FISH & RICE** they excel at keeping it wallet friendly without compromising quality. The name pretty much says it all with a variety of sushi and poke bowls that are based off of, you guessed it, fish and rice.

The space itself is tucked around the corner from the more bustling NW 23rd Avenue. In an area where most dining rooms have as many chairs packed in as possible, Fish & Rice manages to feel spacious. Take your pick of the different-sized tables, some perfect for a small group and others meant to accommodate larger parties or to be used as communal tables.

Choose from a handful of Japanese beers and whiskeys, but the best choice would be to include one of the interesting varieties of sake. Not sure if you like something with more grassy notes and a forward palate punch

TIP

Bring the little ones as there are activities to keep them and the biggest of kids preoccupied; they will find a Super Nintendo that is free to all guests plopped in the middle of the dining room, as well as contemporary and classic comics like *Calvin & Hobbes*.

or creamier mouth-feel and muted acids? The well-versed staff can point you in the right direction.

Lunchtime offerings include a "Choose Two" deal where guests can pick two rolls to go with a salad and a cup of soup for only $13, but the deals are not just for the daytime crowd. For a steal of a deal, individuals can order an *omakase* (chef-selected) tasting for $35! Should you want more control over what is coming your way, be sure to order at least one of their specialty rolls. The Kauai offers shrimp, mango, and spicy yellowtail avocado and is topped with crispy sweet potato shoestrings, and also includes a pineapple salad that is far from traditional but balanced. Their Paper Lantern sets itself apart using Oregon albacore served *tataki* style (seared rare and sliced thinly) with shrimp, red pepper, avocado, radish sprouts, soy paper, and hoisin-Thai chili sauce to add a little bit of sweetness. Whatever roll you get, none come with institutional, Play-Doh texture wasabi; instead find a far creamier dollop that spreads more evenly leaving a consistent amount of heat. Fish & Rice breaks the mold without breaking your bank account.

2

BHUNA

BHUNA is a casual, soulful Indian restaurant focusing on chef-owner Deepak Kaul's family roots. He immigrated to the United States with his family in 1980, and after graduating college found his true calling in the culinary arts. After working 20 years for other people in New York City, London, and San Francisco, Kaul decided to go into business himself highlighting the soulful cuisine of his family's heritage, focusing on the Kashmir region of India. Starting as a pop-up, Bhuna quickly morphed into the brick and mortar spot it is today. Take the fine-dining attention to detail cultivated from Kaul's career, put that focus on a deeply personal cuisine, and

serve it in a casual, approachable setting and you have Bhuna. Take your taste buds on a deep journey as you taste the complex layers to each sauce, perfectly seasoned proteins, and vegetables. Pop in for happy hour to snag their "Beer and a Bowl" deal, which despite the legality of cannabis here, is not a deal on getting baked and drinking, but instead a pint of any beer on tap paired with one of their signature rice bowls. Should you feel like sticking to some smaller snacks, we recommend the chickpea-crusted calamari, a gluten-free take on the classic fried calamari appetizer, served alongside your choice of tamarind sauce or cilantro-mint chutney. For those familiar with Indian cuisine, as well as newbies, Bhuna is a great spot to go when searching for something delicious.

3

THE WAITING ROOM

The doctor can take their sweet time getting back to us if this is the waiting room we get to hang out in. Just half a block off of the bustling NW 23rd Avenue in the Nob Hill neighborhood, chefs Thomas Dunklin and Kyle Rourke serve up Louisiana fried chicken, Pacific Northwest oysters, and an ever-changing menu of small plates and sides at **THE WAITING ROOM**. Poutine gets the first class treatment, swapping out seasoned curly fries for the regular spuds and topping the whole mess with foie gras and Fresno chiles. Bar snacks like fried pickles have a science-defying ability to have a crispy cornmeal batter that is more secure than Fort Knox

when it comes to retaining the moisture of each pickle slice it coats.

With craft cocktails, well-done classics like an Old Fashioned, sparkling wine, and a canned and draft beer selection, there is an adult drink for all the big kids to enjoy. A friendly warm environment with outdoor seating when weather permits allows for tons of different vantage points from this unique dining setting in a retrofitted house. All medical office jokes aside, the name actually stems from a Fugazi song, and the DIY punk culture culminates in a different way here as most of the construction and aesthetics were built by Dunklin and Rourke themselves. They built the spot, they built the flavors, they built our trust in telling you that those other spots can wait, go here.

4 MOBERI

MOBERI is a health-focused cafe that offers a variety of dairy-free acai bowls, smoothies, and oatmeals to give you the energy to make the most out of today. Would you believe it if we told you that this expanding Portland company started with owner Ryan Carpenter selling smoothies from his house made with a blender powered by a bicycle? You should, because that's how it went down! Weird, but hey, that is Portland in a nutshell. A lot of health-focused establishments can make you feel like you showed up to a pop quiz without doing your homework, while Moberi makes health food approachable for everyone, and somehow makes your healthy meal taste like a guilty pleasure. References to '90s pop culture are heavy throughout the menu. Reminisce about the original *Point Break* while sipping a Johnny Utah. Your taste buds will be saying "have mercy!" after tasting the Uncle Jesse Acai Bowl. Leave your guilt at the door because their plant-based desserts will satisfy your sweet tooth without sacrificing flavor. If this concept tickles a memory when you have yet to visit Drip City, it's most likely because you saw the episode of *Shark Tank* where this business went swimming with the sharks; while no one took a bite out of Moberi on the show, everyone in this town seems to be taking a bite out of this menu. The sharks may have lost out, but if you hit up Moberi you'll feel like a winner.

5

LIFE OF PIE

There may not be any tigers in life rafts at this neighborhood pizza shop, but their $5 Margherita pizza happy hour deal is a beast in itself. One whole 12-inch pizza is only $5 every day from 11 a.m. to 6 p.m., among other great options. Share a pie and two beers and walk out for less than 20 bucks. Crowds can form as the office workers finish for the day and an influx of people descend from the surrounding offices. **LIFE OF PIE**'s confident and friendly staff keep the line moving at this second location and the kitchen slings out delicious, affordable pizza out of an eye-catching wood-fired oven. Should you not make it during happy hour, prices are still reasonable with pizzas in the $10 to $15 range for their house specialties, or choose to build your own. Both options offer some of the Pacific Northwest's most recognizable producers for their toppings like Olympia Provisions

and Mama Lil's Peppers. A handful of salads and fresh spaghettis round out the menu, with even the option for gluten-free pasta. No matter what your choice, the love and pride for their product shines in every bite that owner Jason Kallingal and his team put out.

Make sure to have a bottle of their signature chili oil handy when you dine in; the addictive add-on gives every bite that extra kick!

THE BONUS DISTILLERY ROW CRAWL

1. **FREELAND SPIRITS,** 2671 NW Vaughn St., (971) 279-5692, freelandspirits.com

2. **ARIA PORTLAND DRY GIN,** 2304 NW Savier St., ariagin.com

3. **BULL RUN DISTILLING COMPANY,** 2259 NW Quimby St., (503) 224-3483, bullrundistillery.com

4. **WILD ROOTS SPIRITS,** 77 NE Grand Ave., Ste. F, (971) 254-4617, wildrootsspirits.com

5. **WESTWARD WHISKEY,** 65 SE Washington St., (503) 235-3174, westwardwhiskey.com

6. **NEW DEAL DISTILLING AND TASTING ROOM,** 900 SE Salmon St., (503) 234-2513, newdealdistillery.com

7. **ROLLING RIVER SPIRITS,** 1215 SE 8th Ave., Ste. H, (503) 236-3912, rollingriverspirits.com

8. **STRAIGHTAWAY,** 901 SE Hawthorne Blvd., (971) 258-1627, straightawaycocktails.com

9. **EASTSIDE DISTILLING,** 1512 SE 7th Ave., (503) 926-7060, eastsidedistilling.com

10. **STONE BAR BRANDYWORKS,** 3315 SE 19th St., Ste. B, (503) 341-2227, stonebarnbrandyworks.com

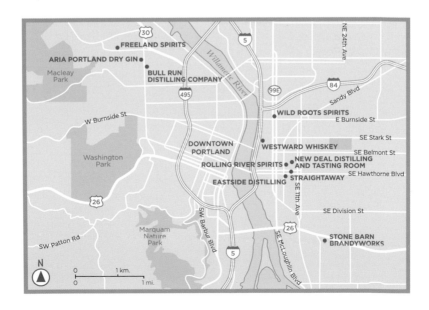

Bonus Crawl!

Distillery Row

THE JOURNEY TO HIT UP ALL THE SMALL-BATCH DISTILLERS and taste the spirits and elixirs that they each excel at actually stretches from the west side of Portland, across the Willamette River, to the Southeast, also known as Distillery Row. All of these creators have included tasting rooms for the public to come in, learn more about how everything is made, taste, and take home a bottle of what you like. The third Saturday of every month, the distilleries feature their version of the same cocktail and donate all proceeds from the sale of that drink to a different local nonprofit every month. Makes for an even better reason to hop around town enjoying cocktails knowing that you are doing good by drinking. With an explosion of distillers making world-class spirits in Oregon for the first time since the Prohibition era, it is easy to see how people love to support all things local in the City of Roses.

1

FREELAND SPIRITS

One of the few women-owned distilleries, **FREELAND SPIRITS** offers small-batch, hand-crafted booze that epitomizes the "less is more" mantra. Beginning with a sole focus on gin, they expanded their offerings to bourbon as well as Geneva, also known as Dutch gin, only offering something new after perfecting it. Childhood best friends Jill Kuehler and Jessica Brantley's teenage babysitting business may not have thrived,

but they and master distiller Molly Troupe are killing the spirits game. With the gorgeously decorated tasting room that offers large windows showing fantastic views of production, we could not ask for a better setting to see some makers in action.

2

ARIA PORTLAND DRY GIN

Enter the clean, modernly decorated tasting room of **ARIA** to find their latest distillations available for the tasting, as well as a curated selection of items to step up your home bar game from some of the city's best makers. Grab glassware from Bull in China, bar tools, and a variety of mixers to take home with a bottle. Two different tasting flights are available for $10 each; taste the reserves or have the current cocktail flight.

3

BULL RUN DISTILLING COMPANY

Founder and master distiller Lee Medoff had made some pretty standout drinks for a lot of big names around town before opening **BULL RUN**. Originally a brewer at local juggernaut McMenamins, Medoff expanded to winemaking and eventually distilling, creating spirits for Aviation Gin as well as Medoyeff Vodka. Branching out on his own, he first focused on pure malt Oregon whiskey; Bull Run Distillery was born. Offering a variety of whiskeys from single malt

to bourbon, now they also have Medoyeff Vodka as well as an aquavit in production for purchase. It is hard to get more local than Bull Run, born and raised in Oregon and creating and showcasing some of Oregon's most distinct spirits.

4

WILD ROOTS SPIRITS

For those that like it fruity, **WILD ROOTS SPIRITS** is your spot. What started as Wild Roots Vodka has expanded into liqueurs, gins, and other concoctions infused with fruits local to the Pacific Northwest and renamed itself Wild Roots Spirits. The Marionberry vodka uses a blackberry derivative created by Oregon State University to infuse a sweetness that truly is Oregon in each bottle. No artificial flavors or colors are used; instead they use over a pound of real fruit in each bottle.

5

WESTWARD WHISKEY

Using the best quality ingredients and taking a minimalist approach to preparation, **WESTWARD WHISKEY** lets the product shine on its own without any parlor tricks. While the name may seem like they just specialize in one spirit, guests can try their gin, vodka, aquavit, and rum in addition to their signature single malt whiskey. Point your wagons westward and head here for a good time.

6 NEW DEAL DISTILLING AND TASTING ROOM

Founded in 2004, not only is **NEW DEAL** the oldest distillery in Portland proper, but it was the first distillery in what is now Distillery Row. Known for its award-winning gin and vodka, guests can come in, buy a bottle, do a tasting, or even take a whiskey-making class from owner and distiller Tom Burkleaux. The Hot Monkey vodka is so hot right now.

7 ROLLING RIVER SPIRITS

The Rickard family's Scandinavian heritage can be found in their production of aquavit. The hand-carved mahogany bar is formed into the shape of a ship's hull, adding to the artistic touches found throughout the tasting room. **ROLLING RIVER SPIRITS** owners Rick and Joan Rickard distill every day with son and daughter Tim and Elizabeth, truly making this a family affair. In addition to aquavit, additional spirits like their gin, vodkas, and whiskey can be tasted onsite.

8 STRAIGHTAWAY

Love you some classic cocktails, but just can't get it together behind the bar? Go directly to **STRAIGHTAWAY**, where they focus on bottled craft cocktails that are good to go: no mixing required. They offer popular drinks so guests can choose to get the party started with no additional equipment required. Sample cute cocktails on a cute lazy Susan, in one of the cutest tasting rooms in all of Distillery Row. Bar snacks that pair perfectly with each cocktail are offered should you get hungry.

9 EASTSIDE DISTILLING

What was once a tiny company has now expanded to a publicly traded company with the goal of bringing smaller-batch companies to the masses. By acquiring a bunch of smaller companies, as well as a bottling and packaging facility, **EASTSIDE DISTILLING** allows many distinct distillers an opportunity to expand their reach. Taste everything from vodkas, gins, whiskeys, and even tequila from their portfolio in their Southeast Portland tasting room. Each distiller creates a product that stands on its own, including some award winners like Redneck Riviera Whiskey, which took the gold medal at the Los Angeles International Spirit Awards.

10 STONE BAR BRANDYWORKS

Husband and wife team Sebastian and Erika Degens are changing people's views about brandy in Portland one distillation at a time at **STONE BAR BRANDYWORKS**. Their warehouse tasting room offers barrel-aged whiskeys, liqueurs, grappa (the grape-based brandy that is all the rage in Italy), as well as European-style brandies that feature local fruit that change with the seasons. Try unique concoctions like Cherry Matsutake or Pacific Northwest Plum that were distilled at the peak of their ripeness to extract the most flavor.

Index

About the Authors

NICOLE GITENSTEIN and her husband, chef **ERIC GITENSTEIN**, are co-owners of tiny Portland restaurant MF Tasty. Keep up with all the special events at @mftasty. Nicole blogs about Portland food and her adventures at MrsMFTasty.com and shares her best eats around town at @mrs.mftasty.